I really BET you CAN!

Anglais 6e
Cycle 3 A1>A2
ÉDITION 2021
Actualisée et enrichie

Sous la direction de

Michelle Jaillet
IA-IPR

Frédéric André
Professeur agrégé
Formateur INSPE
Collège Victor Grignard (69)

Frédérique Denoix-Smart
Professeure certifiée
Formatrice et chargée de mission d'inspection
Collège Marcel Aymé (01)

Anne Doublet
Professeure agrégée
Formatrice INSPE
Lycée de l'Elorn (29)

Guillaume Ogier
Professeur certifié
Formateur INSPE
Interlocuteur académique pour le numérique (IAN)
Collège du portail rouge (42)

Remerciements à M. Lee Smart, BA (Hons) French, agrégé d'anglais, pour sa relecture.

MAGNARD

Direction éditoriale : Alexia Zoulas
Édition (2021) : Marie Chochon
Création graphique et mise en page : Cécile Chaumet
Création graphique couverture : Cécile Chaumet
Iconographie : Véronique Billiotte et Marie-Laure Fior
Illustrations : Mathieu Maillefer *(Story Time)*, Léa Fabre (*Words & Sounds*), Claire Delvaux (rituels et scènes de classe), Nans Grall (*Grammar*, p. 49 et p. 80), Anna Bishop (p. 19-20), Olivier Le Discot (p. 40 et 140)
Cartes : Jenny Wren (gardes) ; Légendes Cartographie (p. 108)
Animations du *Story Time* : Mathieu Maillefer
Chef de projet numérique : Dominique Garrigues
Enregistrements : Pierre Rochet et Vincent Henquinet (EuroDVD)
Enregistrements des chansons : Ives Grimonprez et Guillaume Ogier
L'éditeur adresse ses vifs remerciements à toutes les personnes qui ont participé aux chansons : Vincent Aubrun, Laurent de Carvalho, Boris Lebas, Flavie Aubrun et Jean-Luc Garcia.

5, allée de la 2e D.B. 75015 Paris
www.magnard.fr

ISBN : 978-2-210-11559-0

I Bet You Can pronounce

Les consonnes

/ʃ/ sheep

/tʃ/ chair

/h/ hat

/θ/ mouth
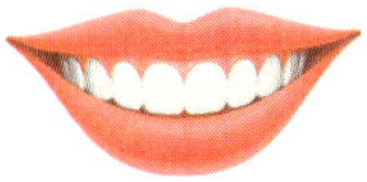

/ð/ mother

/ʒ/ television

/dʒ/ jeans

/ŋ/ ring

/j/ uniform

Les voyelles

/ɪ/ fish

/iː/ key

/e/ pen

/ɔː/ door

/ɒ/ dog

/ə/ banana

/ɜː/ bird

/ʊ/ book

/uː/ shoe

/æ/ cat

/ɑː/ car

/ʌ/ cup

Les diphtongues

/ɪə/ ear
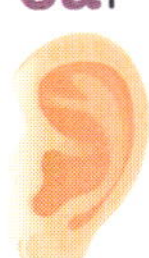

/eə/ bear

/ʊə/ tourist

/eɪ/ day

/aɪ/ eye

/ɔɪ/ boy

/əʊ/ nose

/aʊ/ house

English is music!

Les éditions Magnard remercient chaleureusement **l'ensemble des enseignants ayant participé à des études** sur notre méthode. Leurs avis nous ont été précieux !

C. Alderigi, Annot (04); M-P. Allègre, Bellerive-sur-Allier (03); V. Alliot, Faches-Thumesnil (59); S. Alquier, Billom (63); C. Andre-Riveccie, Lyon (69); E. Antoine, Ribeauville (68); S. Arabdioui, Niort (79); M. Arnould, Fabrègues (34); F. Aumaire Grevet, Claye-Souilly (77); S. Bacon, Nantes (44); O. Barbelet, Reims (51); N. Barret-Protteau, Parthenay (79); M. Baucomont, Bons-en-Chablais (74); M. Belaouinat, Grâces (22); C. Belle, Saint-Didier-sur-Chalaronne (01); A. Berard, La Buisse (38); K. Bernet, Bordeaux (33); E. Biziere, La Rochelle (17); D. Blanchais, Courdimanche (95); S. Bodeux, Bourg-en-Bresse (01); E. Bogé, Gueux (51); V. Boizot, Marans (17); A. Bombois, Saint-Laurent-de-Mûre (69); G. Bonnaud, Leyment (01); D. Bonny, Le Kremlin Bicêtre (94); V. Bony, Saint-Just-Saint-Rambert (42); N. Borrione, Villeparisis (77); C. Bréham, Menucourt (95); N. Brouk, Avignon (84); E. Caille, Nantes (44); A. Calipel, Clermont-Ferrand (63); L. Cappoen, Annoeullin (59); E. Caretti, Montbéliard (25); S. Carvalho, Vélines (24); A. Cassar, Lésigny (77); V. Castel, Saint-Brieuc (22); F. Castillo, Perpignan (66); A. Catta, Harfleur (76); X. Chabierski, Lille (59); Y. Chaland, Feurs (42); C. Charroin-Thouilly, Saint-Bonnet-le-Château (42); S. Chastel, Boissy-Saint-Léger (94); P. Chaubard, Paris (75); A. Chossière, Saint-Just-Saint-Rambert (42); H. Chupin, Saint-Benoît (974); S. Colle, Juniville (08); A. Collet-Coquemont, Mormant (77); S. Colussi, La Force (24); U. Corneiller, Valence (26); S. Creuzet, Saint-Pourçain-sur-Sioule (03); G. Cribier, Brissac-Loire-Aubance (49); O. Dagueneau, Longpre-les-Corps-Saints (80); L. Daubié-Challant, Giromagny (90); S. Dautrey, Sassenage (38); I. De La Croix, Lecci (2A); A. Delporte, Thairé (17); V. Demay-Potier, Livry-Gargan (93); C. Demol, Lesquin (59); N. Dergham, Saint-Étienne (42); C. Desloges, Heiltz-le-Maurupt (51); S. Druelle, Saultain (59); F. Duffait, Morteau (25); A. Dupau, Tartas (40);F. Duperray, Saint-André-de-Corcy (01); R. Duquesnoy, Colombes (92); B. El Amri Courtois, Montpellier (34); P. Engelmann, Andernos (33); M-J. Fabrizy, Calvi (2B); C. Farges, Rennes (35); P. Fernandes, Tarnos (40); L. Ferrer-Guillaume, Gennevilliers (92); M. Ferry, Bénaménil (54); B. Fleutot, Honfleur (14); K. Fort, Carcassonne (11); C. Fournier, La Queue-en-Brie (94); M. Fox, Saint-Vit (25); M-P. Foy, Romilly-sur-Seine (10); N. Garden, Chassieu (69); N. Gauthier, Parthenay (79); W. Gautier, Beaumont-le-Roger (27); C. Gendrin, Nantes (44); G. Gerbeau, Boissy-Saint-Léger (94); H. Ges, Andernos (33); A. Gobin, Chatellerault (86); F. Gonneau, Mulsanne (72); D. Grange, Craponne (69); A. Guena, Saint-Germain-en-Laye (78); B. Guilhon, Greasque (13); Y. Guillen Barnett, Nantes (44); P. Hattais, Lyon (69); G. Hegney, Montrevel-en-Bresse (01); A. Humbert, Chambray-lès-Tours (37); A. Hurisse, Chatou (78); S. Jacquy, Faremoutiers (77); C. Jeanne, Reyrieux (01); D. Jouenne, Saint-Lô (50); I. Karas, Evreux (27); A. Lacouture, Saint-Martin-le-Vinoux (38); C. Laffont, Trévoux (01); L. Lanoës, Châtelaillon-Plage (17); C. Lasala, Marseille (13); B. Lavercher, Lesquin (59); S. Le Louet, Guichen (35); G. Léandri, Saint-Just-en-Chaussée (60); N. Lebon, Charleville-Mézières (08); M. Leduc, Lagny-sur-Marne (77); V. Liabeuf, Anse (69); S. Lopez, Aujols (46); S. Lorho, Lorient (56); S. Lovisa, Vincennes (94); M. Lugenbuhler, Belfort (90); V. Magot, Lentilly (69); J. Malleron, Les Mureaux (78); A. Mamou, Carcassonne (11); E. Marcon, Veauche (42); P. Margarito, Montrevel-en-Bresse (01); C. Marti, Perpignan (66); C. Martin, Valence (26); A. Meffre, Aramon (30); M. Meira, Romilly-sur-Seine (10); C. Melle Grychta, Billom (63); D. Mery, Mordelles (35); C. Miffre, Cabestany (66); J. Miot, Saint-Denis-en-Val (45); K. Morgan, Saint-Laurent-en-Grandvaux (39); D. Moulenat-Batlle, Cabestany (66); O. Mrula, Bouilly (10); F. Muller, Villeneuve-lès-Maguelone (34); A. Nadaud, Miribel (01); E. Ohlmer, Lésigny (77); T. Okio, Neuville-sur-Saône (69); A. Olivré, Brest (29); A. Paget, La Norville (91); A. Paniel, Villemoisson-sur-Orge (91); H. Parizot, La Fare-les-Oliviers (13); M. Parsy, Saint-Valery-sur-Somme (80); I. Paschetta, Calvi (2B); J. Pécoil, Vergt (24); S. Peharpre, Offranville (76); B. Philippot, Neufchef (57); F. Pierre, Quintin (22); R. Pinto, Perpignan (66); D. Plantier, Saint-Claude (971); A. Pommier, Lyon (69); C. Pompey, Boën-sur-Lignon (42); M. Pourrère, Amou (40); A. Quesnel, Rouen (76); P. Rahoult, Paris (75); A. Reboul, Sorgues (84); A. Retournay, Bayon (54); A. Roussey, Bar-sur-Seine (10); FR. Saber, Venissieux (69); A-S. Saint-Sulpice, Trévoux (01); M. Schilling, Livry-Gargan (93); N. Seghier, Grenoble (38); N. Séguy, Forcalquier (04); D. Septfontaine, Ris Orangis (91); E. Stéfanini, Marcillat (03); G. Tisseur-Ragueneau, Feurs (42); A. Tommasini, Charleville-Mézières (08); A. Toth, Niort (79); M. Trichet, Le Mesnil-Saint-Denis (78); C. Urset Chiesa, Tarare (69); O. Verscheure, Saint-Bonnet-le-Château (42); E. Viet, Juniville (08); A. Vignol, Chartres (28); M. Vivien, Chantonnay (85); C. Weber, Mourmelon-le-Grand (51); S. Wilmot-Hall, Castelnau-le-Lez (34)

Bienvenue dans ton manuel !

Découvrir une langue, c'est découvrir un nouveau monde

- Ce manuel t'ouvre la porte du **monde anglo-saxon** : vie quotidienne, personnalités anglophones, lieux géographiques, légendes, coutumes, héros et héroïnes ...
- Tu découvriras aussi une famille britannique un peu spéciale, les Jones... Ce sera peut-être ta première **série animée** en **version originale** (*Story Time*).

Parler « vrai » !

- Ce manuel t'offre une **langue authentique**.
- Le travail sur la **prononciation** est très important. Parler anglais, c'est presque... chanter !
- Les **tâches** à réaliser sont **motivantes** : elles correspondent à de **vraies situations** de la vie d'un élève ou d'une classe britannique.

Pratiquer une langue vivante tous les jours

- Les **outils numériques** te permettent de t'entraîner à la maison ou au CDI : écoute les MP3 00 et fais les Activités Interactives.
- Dans le **Workbook**, tu trouveras aussi de nombreuses activités pour progresser de manière ludique.

Développer ta confiance en toi et progresser sereinement

- Ce manuel prend en compte les **acquis du primaire** tout en proposant des situations de communication simples pour **poser les bases** (*Re-Cycle!*).
- Les *Lessons* proposent des **apprentis-sages progressifs**, avec de nombreuses aides (*Help!*).
- Le **rythme de progression** de chacun est respecté, tout en encourageant la **collaboration** entre les élèves (AP).

En fin d'année, tu pourras **valider le niveau A1**... et même **A2** dans quelques activités langagières !

Have a fantastic year!
We *really* know you can!

Les auteurs

Sommaire

Visite guidée de ton manuel !

Ouverture

- Les **compétences** à développer dans l'unité.
- La **tâche finale** que tu réaliseras.
- Une **chanson originale** pour démarrer en musique !

Re-cycle!

- Des activités progressives pour **réviser efficacement** ce que tu as appris à l'école primaire et dans ton manuel.

Lesson 1 "Discover"/"Go further"

- " Discover " Découvre la **culture anglophone** !
- Des **activités** progressives autour de documents **authentiques** : vidéo, audio, textes, photos…
- " Go further " **Poursuis ta découverte** de la **culture anglophone** avec des affiches, tableaux, *comics*…

Lesson 2 "Story Time"

- Le **plaisir** d'un **vrai dessin animé** : les aventures des Jones, une famille de **superhéros / héroïnes britanniques**.
- Pour **rêver, imaginer, jouer** des **rôles** en anglais.

Play... (AP)

- Dans chaque unité, un **jeu** collectif **différent**.
- Quand on dialogue et qu'on collabore en anglais avec ses camarades, **jouer c'est apprendre** !

Help Yourself! (AP)

- Des activités variées pour **progresser à l'oral** et **à l'écrit**.
- Un **choix** de **documents** de **niveaux différents**, signalés par des **étoiles**.
- Des **conseils** et **stratégies** pour prendre **confiance en toi** et **réussir**.

Language Lab, Words and Sounds

- Tout le **lexique** de l'unité réuni pour faciliter la **mémorisation** des mots et de leur **prononciation**.

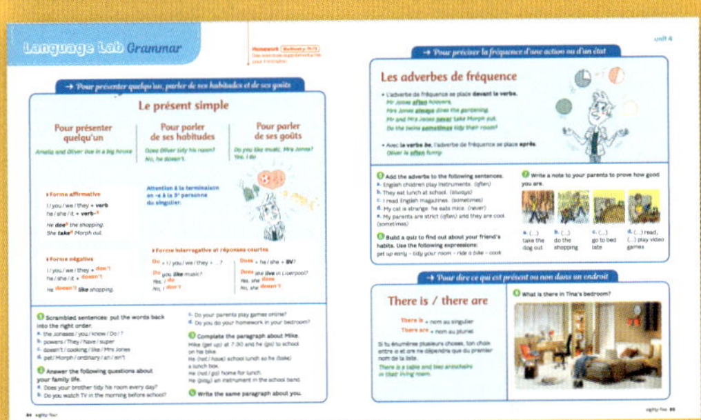

Language Lab, Grammar

- Les notions de **grammaire** expliquées **simplement** et en contexte, avec des exemples.

Final Task

- Des **tâches motivantes** et originales, pour développer **l'autonomie** et le **travail de groupe**.
- Sois **créatif(ve)** et suis les étapes, pas à pas.

Et dans ton Workbook ...

Les renvois au Workbook sont signalés par Workbook p. 00

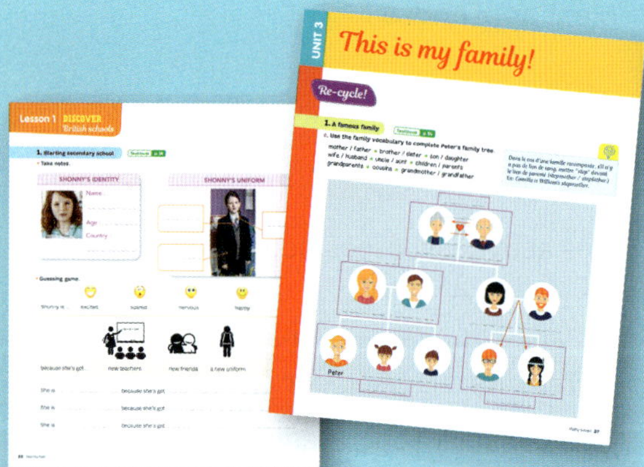

Des supports pour prendre en notes ce que tu entends dans les **documents audio et vidéo**, et pour travailler en classe.

Dans les séances d'"accompagnement personnalisé" (AP), tu pourras travailler **à ton rythme**.

Les **fiches AP** de ton workbook t'aident à développer tes compétences à l'écrit et à l'oral. **Chaque fiche correspond à un niveau du CECRL.**

⭐ = A1

⭐⭐ = A1 vers A2

⭐⭐⭐ = A2

Tu peux choisir la fiche et le document que tu veux travailler, et progresser à ton rythme.

Des activités pour **mémoriser le lexique**. Tu peux écouter tous les mots grâce aux MP3 00 .

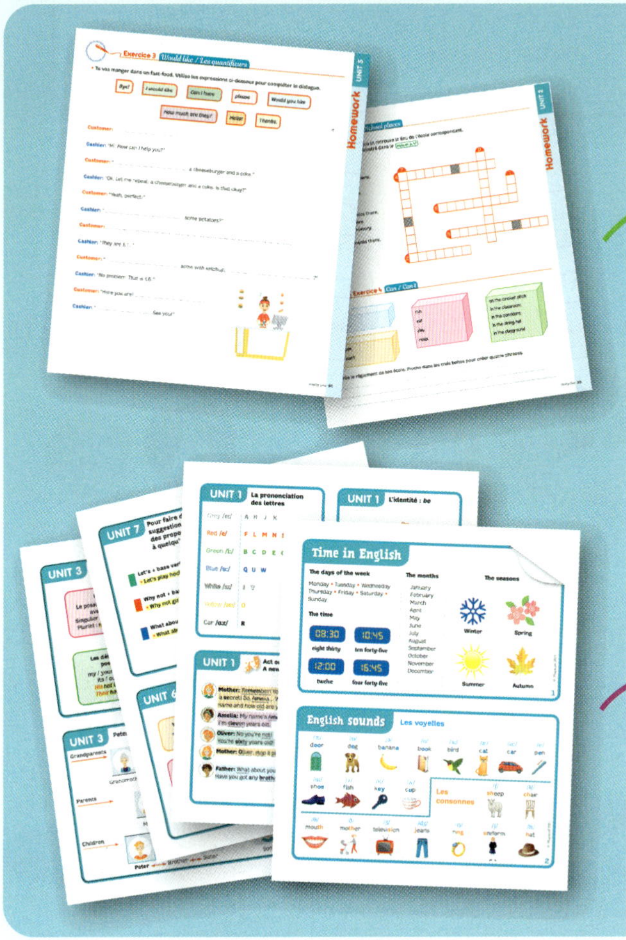

Des **exercices** pour travailler en **autonomie** et réviser les acquis (*Homework*).

À la fin de ton Workbook, tu trouveras **22 stickers**, à coller au fur et à mesure de l'année dans ton cahier d'anglais quand ton/ta professeur(e) te l'indiquera.

Comprendre les pictogrammes de ton manuel

Les activités langagières

- Écouter et comprendre
- Lire et comprendre
- Parler en continu
- Réagir et dialoguer
- Écrire et réagir à l'écrit

Les supports numériques pour l'élève

(accès en un clic dans le manuel numérique élève ou sur le site compagnon)

MP3 00 Document audio

MP4 00 Document vidéo

Pupils' Interactive Activities — Activités interactives

Les supports pour ton/ta professeur(e) :

Audio 00 / Video 00 / TEACHER'S SLIDES — Documents pour la classe

Les dessins animés du Story TIME

Principales compétences :

- Utiliser des indices sonores et visuels pour déduire le sens.
- Suivre le fil d'une histoire simple.
- Acquérir des repères culturels.

Meet the Jones clan...

Mrs and Mr Jones
Des parents pas comme les autres...

Amelia and Oliver Jones
Des jumeaux au caractère bien trempé !

Sophia and Tim
De vrais amis

Morph
un animal un peu spécial...

QUESTION :
Faut-il voir tous les épisodes pour suivre ?

RÉPONSES :
Si tu en as raté un, pas de problème :

- Grâce à cette page tu connais les personnages.
- Comme dans les séries, il y a un « *Previously* » en début de chaque épisode.

... and the others.

Nosy Parker
Un journaliste « fouineur » qui traque le secret des Jones...

Bully and Slimy
Des camarades de classe dont il faut se méfier...

Ce que dit le programme :

« C'est l'exposition régulière et quotidienne à la langue qui favorise les progrès » !

Les Activités interactives pour l'élève

Pupils' Interactive Activities

...

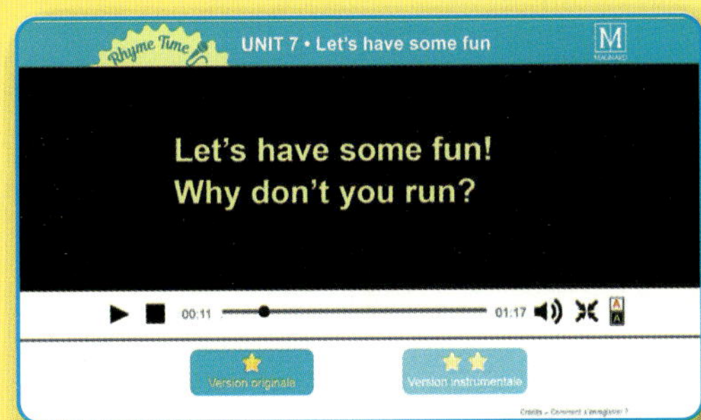

Karaokés

Tu aimes le rock, la pop et le rap ?

Découvre 7 chansons inédites inspirées de grands courants musicaux anglo-saxons. Chanter, c'est faire sienne la mélodie de l'anglais.

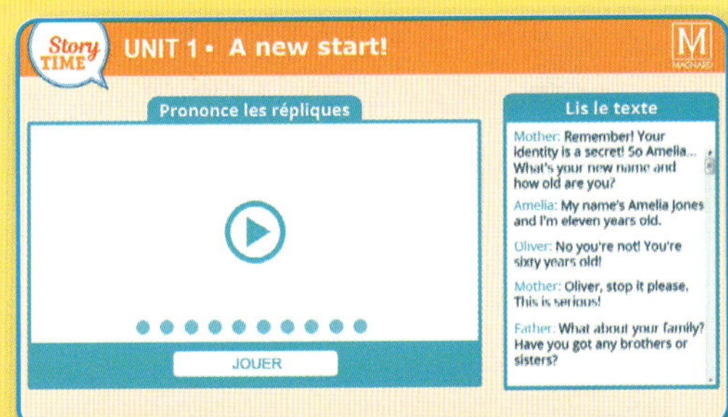

Act out!

Entraîne-toi à imiter les intonations des héros/héroïnes et joue les différents rôles.

Revois les épisodes grâce au code que te donnera ton/ta professeur/e.

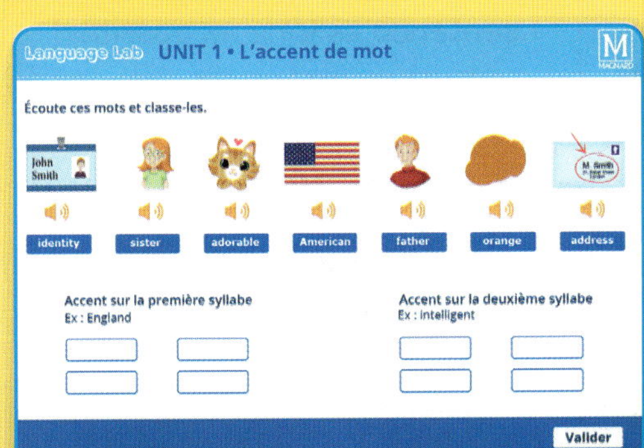

Exercices autocorrectifs

Progresse tout au long de l'année avec les 40 activités de lexique, grammaire et phonologie, en lien avec chaque unité.

QUESTION :
Comment accéder à ces activités ?

RÉPONSES :

▶ En un clic dans le manuel numérique élève.

▶ En allant sur le site compagnon : www.irbyc.ele.site.magnard.fr

Rituels de début de séance

Easy Warming up

1 Let's take the register!

Join in to sit down! Count from 28 to 1 or from 1 to 28.

Pupil A: "twenty-eight, Kevin?"

Kevin: "twenty-seven, Lisa?" etc.

2 What's the date today?

Battle the other team. Give the name(s) of:

- the days of the week
- the days of the weekend
- the first 3 months of the year
- the winter/spring/summer/autumn months

3 Spell the word

Spell a word starting with letter... Listen and continue playing.

Pupil A: "A → a.p.p.l.e"

Pupil B: "Apple. S → s.c.h.o.o.l"

4 What's the weather like today?

Battle the other team! Give the longest weather forecast.

Pupil A: It's sunny!

Pupil B: It's sunny and bright!

Pupil C: It's sunny and bright and it's warm!

Pupil D: It's sunny and bright and it's warm and it's not windy.

sunny cloudy rainy snowy foggy windy hot cold

5 Make chain sentences!

In turn, say a word to make a sentence. Make your sentence as long as possible!

You | are | an | intelligent | pupil | and | ...

6 Play with tongue twisters

Can you say:

- Thin sticks, thick bricks.
- Betty Botter bought some butter.
- She sells seashells on the seashore.
- Peter Piper picked a peck of pickled peppers.
- Red lorry, yellow lorry, red lorry, yellow lorry.
- How much wood would a woodchuck chuck if a woodchuck could chuck wood?

7 Guess the password

Team A agrees on a word (e.g.: an animal).
Team B asks questions to crack the code.

Team B: Is it an animal?
Team A: Yes, it is.
Team B: Does it live in Africa?
Team A: Yes, it does.
Team B: It's an elephant!

8 Play the teacher

1. Start the lesson pretending you are the teacher today.

Take the register, get information about the weather, or choose a game to start the lesson!

2. Give orders!

Pupil A mimicks an order or an interdiction.

Pupil B acts it out.

9 Let's mime actions!

Pupil A mimes an action, pupil B guesses the action.

You're dancing!

10 What did you do?

Pupil A: Did you watch TV yesterday?
Pupil B: Yes, I did / No, I didn't.

go to bed late
organise a party
watch a film
share / send / take a photo
go shopping
visit... (a place / someone)
play football / tennis...
celebrate someone's birthday
chat with your friends

UNIT 1

Who are you?

DANS CETTE UNITÉ

Tu vas découvrir

- Quelques personnalités et pays anglophones
- Le monde de la mystérieuse famille Jones !

Tu seras capable de

- Comprendre l'identité de quelqu'un
- Épeler un mot et le prononcer de manière compréhensible
- Te présenter et présenter une personne (personnalité / famille)
- Interroger quelqu'un sur son identité et sa famille

Et tu vas

First Task ▸ Jouer à trouver ton jumeau dans la classe

Final Task ▸ Créer une galerie de portraits originale

Rhyme Time

Audio 01

MP3 01

Who are you?

1, 2, who are you?
3, 4, open the door,
5, 6, 7, 8, don't, don't be late,
9, 10, take your pen!
11, listen,
12, 13, 14, look at the screen,
15, 16, 17, here comes the Queen!
18, 19, 20, don't be silly!
1, 2, 3, 4, 5, (x2)
6, 7, 8, 9, and 10!
1, 2, who are you?
3, 4, open the door,
5, 6, 7, 8, don't, don't be late,
9, 10, take your pen!

Pupils' Interactive Activities

My Karaoke!
Entraîne-toi à chanter avec ton karaoké !

"Big Hero 6", a Disney animated film

Re-cycle!

Remember?

Compétences
- Épeler des mots familiers.
- Demander et donner des informations sur soi.

1. Letters and colours

a. Listen to the "Funky Alphabet" and sing along. Audio 02 MP3 02

b. Play with the colours. Workbook p. 4

c. Write the letters in the right cloud according to their pronunciation. Workbook p. 5

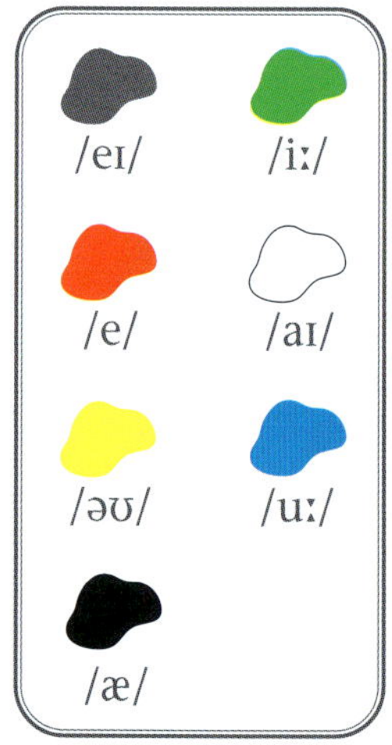

d. Battle your friends: The "Mime-a-letter" challenge.

e. Battle your teacher: The "10-letter" challenge. Together name the ten letters your teacher points at and win the battle!

SCORE
• It's the right letter = 1 point for you
• It's the wrong letter = 1 point for the teacher

2. Wordsearch

Workbook p. 6

a. Choose a grid and find the 17 words.

b. Classify the words of the grid into two categories.

3. I.D., please!

a. Listen to Sherlock Holmes's questions. Audio 03

b. Now match the questions with the pictures below.

1

2

3

4. Play the detective!

Workbook p. 6

Fill in your ID card in your workbook but change your name, your age or your city.
Play the detective, ask your friend questions and find the false information.

Lesson 1 DISCOVER *Identities*

Compétences
- Comprendre des informations simples sur une personne.
- Dialoguer sur les nationalités.

1. The lost passport

a. Get ready to listen.
What information have you got in a passport?

b. Listen to the two dialogues and complete the information for the two passports.

Audio 04-05 Workbook p. 7

c. The policeman has got one passport: is it passport A or passport B?

Help!
This is a policeman. Imagine his questions!

d. Recap the information on the passport.

2. Countries and nationalities

a. Listen, repeat and memorise. Then check your spelling with your teacher. Audio 06 MP3 03 Workbook p. 7

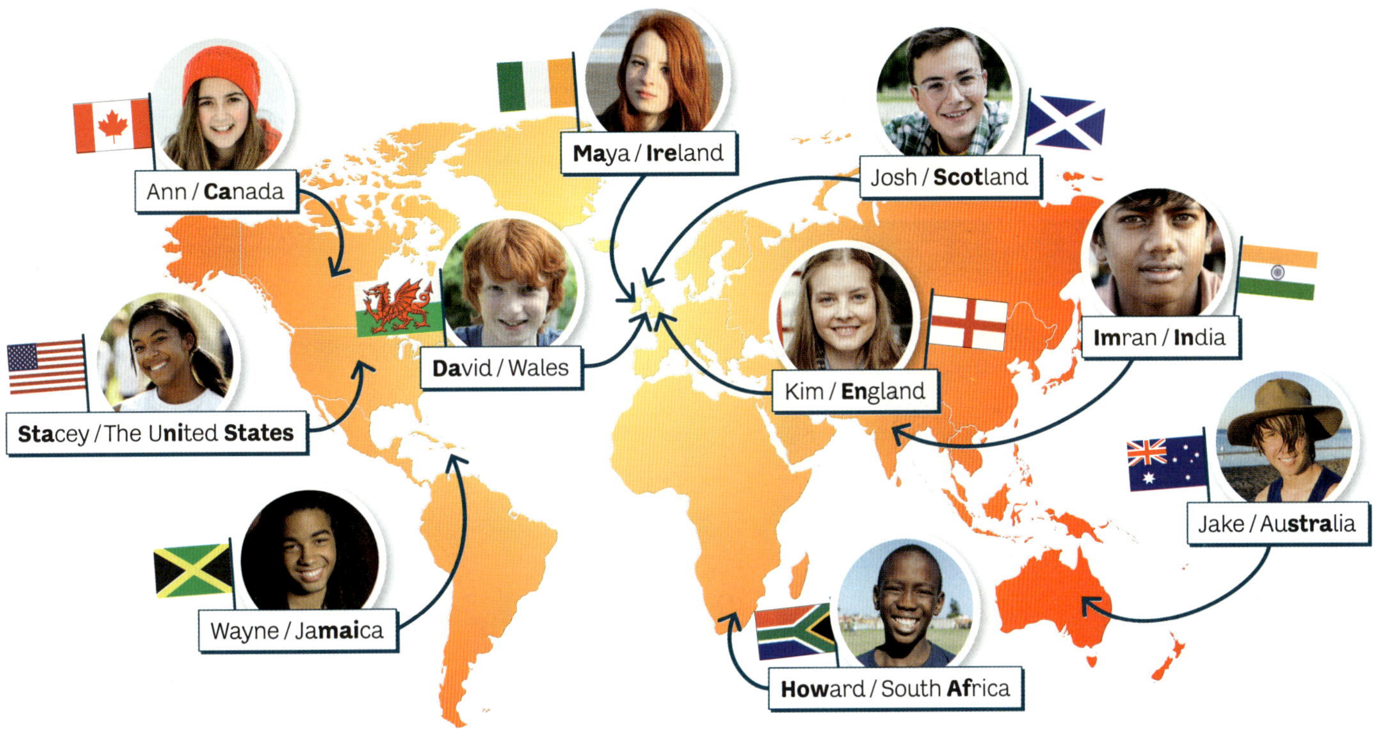

b. Learn about nationalities and their pronunciation. Audio 07-08 MP3 04-05 Workbook p. 8

c. Speak: Guess who I am!

Pupil A: *"My flag is white and red."*
Pupil B: *"So, you're Ann, and you're from Canada."*
Pupil A: *"Yes, you're right."* ✓

Pupil A: *"My flag is white and red."*
Pupil B: *"So, you're Jake, and you're from Australia."*
Pupil A: *"No, you're wrong."* ✗

Help!

England
+ Wales
+ Scotland
= **Great Britain**

3. Find your "twin" in the class!

First Task

Pick a card. Look at your new identity, then go and ask questions in the class to find your "twin"!

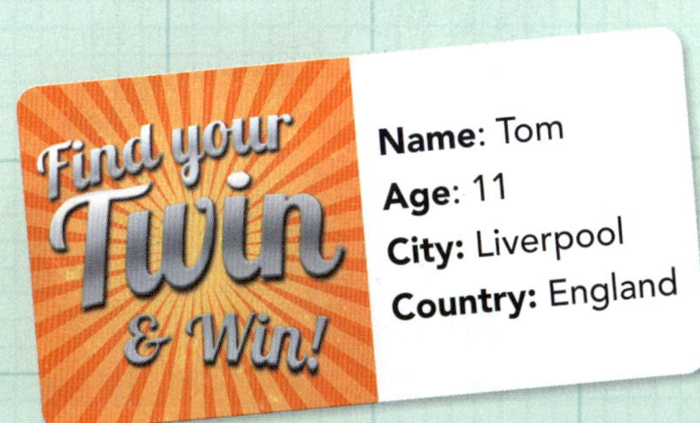

Lesson 1 GO FURTHER
The British love...

Compétences
- Identifier des nationalités.
- Reconnaître les symboles culturels.
- Identifier des personnalités réelles ou fictives.

1. The British love rugby

They are...
They support...

a. Look at the supporters: what is their nationality? Who do they support?

b. Match the national emblems with the pictures. Can you spot two of them in the pictures?

1

2

3

4

NATIONAL EMBLEMS

The English rose 

The Scottish thistle 

The Welsh leek 

The Irish shamrock 

2. Famous characters

a. Who is real? Who is fictional?

b. Complete the texts with the right names:
James Bond – J. K. Rowling – Sherlock Holmes – Elizabeth I.

Lesson 2 Story TIME

Compétences
- Comprendre le portrait d'une famille.
- Décrire simplement la personnalité de quelqu'un.

A new start!

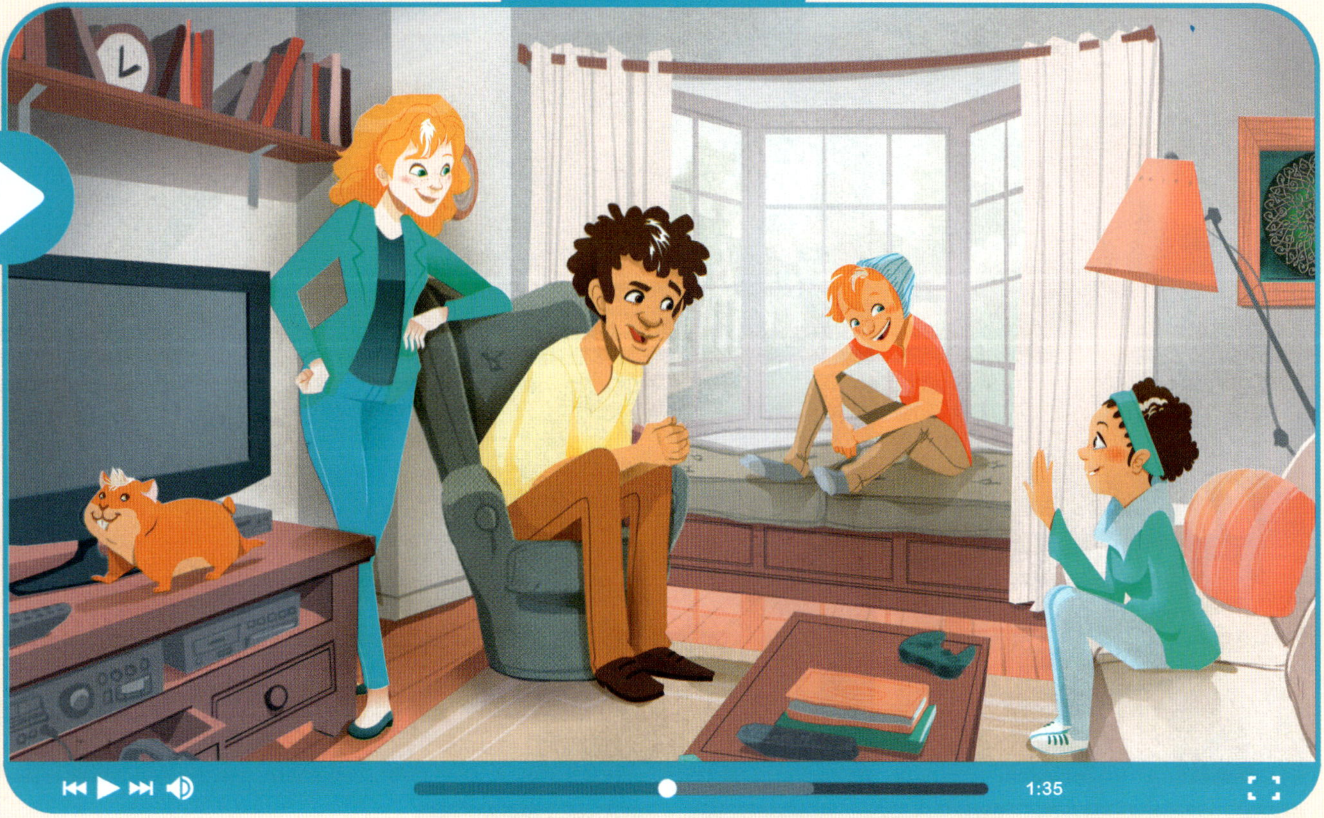

1. Get ready

a. Look at the picture and say what you can.

b. Get ready to watch.

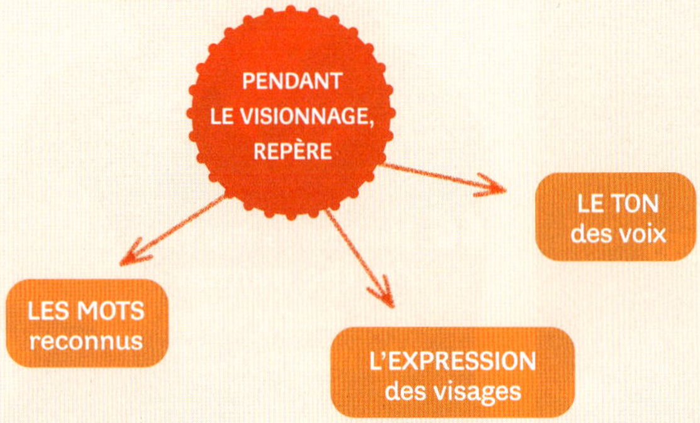

2. Watch the episode

Video 01

a. Take notes about Oliver and Amelia Jones. Workbook p. 9

b. Recap what you know.

3. Act out!

Workbook p. 10

a. Practise acting. MP3 06

b. Memorise and act out the scene.

Pupils' Interactive Activities

Act out!
- Prépare ton rôle avec le karaoké.
- Ton/ta professeur(e) te donnera le code pour revoir l'épisode.

4. Personalities

a. Listen and repeat the adjectives. Audio 09

sporty | **fun**ny | strange | in**tel**ligent | a**dor**able | cre**a**tive

serious | cool | strict | **spe**cial | **sil**ly | **cu**rious

b. Match the adjectives with the family photos.

5. Portrait

a. Choose a family member and write a short presentation. Workbook p. 10

Help!

Oliver is… **and** he is…
Oliver is… **but** he is not…

b. Read your presentation to the class.
Don't use names, use pronouns. Who is it?

Help!

 → he

 → she

 → it

HAVE FUN IN GROUPS

Play "Sounds & Letters"

1. Speaking — Prononcer de manière compréhensible

How to play — 10 min

- Roll the dice and speak! *It's my turn./ It's your turn.*
- Say a word with a similar sound.
- Miss a turn if you speak French!

Snake: Go back 3 spaces.

Ladder: Go up.

Finish here!	Rhyming with fifteen 34	33	"So" 32	A word with three syllables 31	A word with the stress on the 1st syllable: family 30
Rhyming with daddy 24	"Sherlock" 25	"Year" 26	Ending with the letter R 27	"Funny" 28	"Six" 29
23	"Ten" 22	"He" 21	"Three" 20	"Flag" 19	"You" 18
Ending with -ia 12	"They" 13	14	"Brown" 15	"Book" 16	Ending with -ty 17
"Ireland" 11	Beginning with the letter T 10	"Calm" 9	Ending with -land 8	"Hair" 7	6
Start here!	"Five" 1	"Name" 2	"Thanks" 3	Beginning with the letter P 4	A word with the stress on the 2nd syllable: tomorrow 5

Help Yourself!

unit 1 AP

2. Listening Relever des indices et apprendre à les classer

→ En notant les mots que tu reconnais.
→ En les organisant par thèmes (identité, famille...).

MP3 07

MP3 08

MP3 09

Choose a document and go to your workbook.

Workbook p. 11

3. Reading Comprendre un texte court et simple

→ En t'appuyant sur les mots que tu reconnais.
→ En associant les informations aux bonnes personnes.
→ En relevant des indices et en les classant.

Choose a document and go to your workbook.

Ariana Grande

My family is from Italy, but I'm from Florida, USA. I'm young and famous. My hair is long and I have big brown eyes. Justin Bieber is my friend.

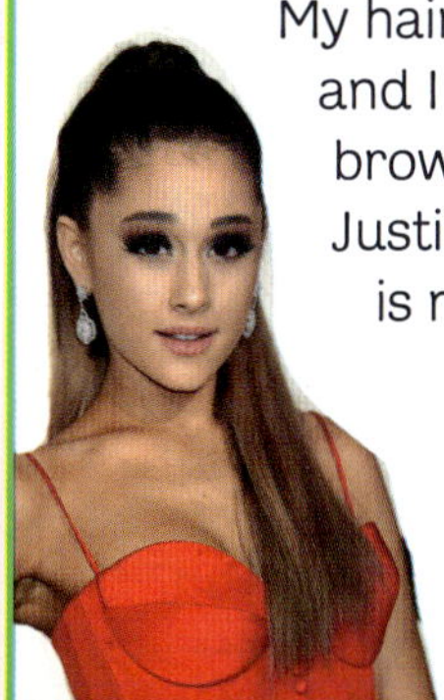

Workbook p. 12

Jaden Smith

I'm American. I'm from Malibu, California. My little sister, Willow, is a singer. She's very eccentric! My dad, Will Smith, is a famous actor. I like martial arts. I'm a rapper and I'm cool.

Workbook p. 12

Millie Bobby Brown

Hi! My name is Millie Bobby Brown. My birthday is on February 19th. I'm not American, I'm English and I live in London and in Atlanta (USA). I have two sisters and one brother. I am an actress, I like boxing and rapping and I love my dogs! I am a Liverpool football team fan.

Workbook p. 13

Pupils' Interactive Activities
Entraîne-toi avec les exercices interactifs.

Memorise the words!

1 Colours
Play with your partner.
Pupil A points at an object,
pupil B says the colour.
Do it as fast as you can!

2 Personality. Guess my word!
★ Pupil A spells a word,
pupil B writes it.

S-P-O-R-T-Y
Sporty!

★★ Pupil A chooses a word but gives only a letter and its rank (*"Letter number 1 is A"*).
Pupil B says the word.

3 Countries. Where is it?
Pupil A gives a city,
pupil B gives the country.

London
England!

Practise!

A Les diphtongues
On parle de **di**phtongues quand le son est composé de **deux** sons voyelles qui se suivent.

1. Écoute, répète et entraîne-toi ! Audio 10 MP3 10

/aɪ/ → white – eyes – write – five – find
/eɪ/ → grey – creative – patient – name – Australia crazy – strange – Jamaica
/aʊ/ → brown – count

2. Lis à haute voix. Quel est l'intrus? Audio 11 MP3 11

a. *address – name – age*
b. *sister – white – twins*
c. *States – family – age*
d. *brown – orange – Scotland*

B L'accent de mot
Les mots en anglais ont un accent tonique. Mais il n'est pas toujours à la même place !

Écoute, répète et entraîne-toi ! Audio 12 MP3 12

Accent sur la 1re syllabe	Accent sur la 2e syllabe
Oliver – **fa**mily **te**lephone – **En**gland **o**range – **Ca**nada	A**me**lia – Aus**tra**lia a**do**rable – to**mo**rrow in**tel**ligent – cre**a**tive **i**dentity – Ja**mai**ca

C L'intonation et les liaisons
Fais attention à l'intonation et aux liaisons entre les mots !

Écoute, répète et entraîne-toi ! Audio 13 MP3 13

What's your **name**?
How old are **you**?
Where are you **from**?
Where do you **live**?

Colours MP3 14

- blue /uː/
- green /iː/
- pink /ɪ/
- **or**ange /ɒ/
- brown /aʊ/
- **yell**ow /əʊ/

- red /e/
- white /aɪ/
- grey /eɪ/
- black /æ/
- **pur**ple /ɜː/

Family MP3 15

- **mo**ther /ʌ/
- **fa**ther /ɑː/
- **bro**ther /ʌ/
- **sis**ter /ɪ/
- twins /ɪ/

parents /eə/ (mother, father)

children /ɪ/ (brother, sister, twins)

Personality MP3 16

- **spor**ty /ɔː/
- **fun**ny /ʌ/
- strange /eɪ/

- in**tel**ligent /e/
- a**dor**able /ɔː/
- **se**rious /ɪə/

- strict /ɪ/
- cool /uː/
- **sil**ly /ɪ/
- cre**a**tive /eɪ/

Identity MP3 17

- **first** name /ɜː/
- name /eɪ/
- **fam**ily /æ/
- ad**dress** /e/

- age /eɪ/
- hair /eə/
- eyes /aɪz/

Countries MP3 18

- The Un**i**ted **King**dom /aɪ/ /ɪ/
- **Eng**land /ən/
- Wales /eɪ/
- **Scot**land /ɒ/

- **Ire**land /aɪə/
- **Ca**nada /æ/
- The Un**i**ted **States** /aɪ/ /eɪ/
- **In**dia /ɪ/

Actions MP3 19

- **lis**ten /ɪ/
- speak /iː/
- read /iː/
- look /ʊ/

- ask /ɑː/
- write /aɪ/
- spell /e/

Language Lab *Grammar*

Homework (Workbook p. 16-19)
Des exercices supplémentaires pour t'entraîner.

→ *Pour se présenter ou présenter quelqu'un*

Be

Sert à :
- donner ton nom, ton âge
- parler de ta personnalité
- dire d'où tu viens

▸ Forme affirmative

Forme pleine	Forme contractée
I **am**	I'**m**
you **are**	you'**re**
he / she / it **is**	he / she / it'**s**
we / you / they **are**	we / you / they'**re**

▸ Forme négative

Forme pleine	Forme contractée
I **am not**	I'**m not**
you **are not**	you **aren't**
he / she / it **is not**	he / she / it **isn't**
we / you / they **are not**	we / you / they **aren't**

▸ Forme interrogative

Am I ...?
Are you ...?
Is he / she / it ...?
Are we / you / they ...?

▸ Réponses brèves

Affirmatives	Négatives
Yes, I **am**.	No, I'**m not**.
Yes, you **are**.	No, you **aren't**.
Yes, he / she / it **is**.	No, he / she / it **isn't**.
Yes, we / you / they **are**.	No, we / you / they **aren't**.

1 Complète les phrases avec le verbe *be*.

a. *Amelia and Oliver ... twins.*
b. *Oliver ... 19 years old.*
c. *I ... in the classroom.*
d. *The USA and Australia ... in Europe.*
e. *The British flag ... red, white and blue.*
f. *I ... from Australia.*
g. *Laurel and Hardy ... American.*
h. *Elsa ... a character from the movie Frozen.*
i. *I ... good at tennis.*

2 Utilise les informations pour présenter Wendy et Bart.

Name	Bart Simpson	Wendy Darling
Age	10	12
City	Springfield	London
Personality	silly, cool, funny	adorable

→ *Pour se désigner ou désigner une ou plusieurs autres personnes*

Les pronoms personnels sujets

- Contrairement au français, **l'anglais ne fait pas la différence entre « tu » et « vous »** (= *you*).
- À la 3e personne du singulier, l'anglais distingue **les personnes** (masculin : *he*, féminin : *she*) **et les objets et animaux** (*it*).

3 Complète avec le bon pronom.

a. *Oliver is 11 years old and … is from Liverpool.*
b. *Oliver and Amelia are brother and sister: … are twins.*
c. *New York is a very big city but … is not the capital of the USA.*
d. *Amelia is Oliver's twin sister and … loves her pet, Morph.*
e. *My English teacher is Mr. Moore: … is British, from Manchester.*
f. *My dog is beautiful. … is black.*

4 Trouve le bon pronom.

a.

b.

c.

d.

e.

f.

→ *Pour se renseigner*

Les mots interrogatifs

What's your name? *My name is Peter.* **How old** are you? *I'm 13.* **Where** are you from? *I'm from the USA.*

5 Trouve le mot interrogatif qui convient pour compléter les questions.

	• *is Amelia's family name?*
How old •	• *are you from?*
What •	• *are you?*
Where •	• *is Liverpool?*
	• *are the colours of the US flag?*

6 Réponds aux questions de l'exercice 5, en utilisant les éléments suivants.

… Jones
… Liverpool
… 12
… in England
… red, white and blue

Final Task

Domaine 2 Socle

Make the funny portrait gallery of the class

Ton projet

Toi et tes camarades, vous allez réaliser une mosaïque originale de portraits des élèves de la classe.

Les étapes à suivre

STEP 1
Introduce yourself!
Présente-toi : nom, âge, ville, famille.

STEP 2
Describe yourself
Décris ta personnalité avec quelques adjectifs.

STEP 3
Practice time
Entraîne-toi à présenter ces informations.

STEP 4
Be creative!
Enregistre ta présentation avec un téléphone / une tablette. Si tu n'as pas d'outil numérique, crée avec tes camarades une mosaïque de portraits (photos ou dessins + textes) à afficher dans la classe et fais une présentation à l'oral.

I BET YOU CAN!

MAINTENANT, TU ES CAPABLE DE :

- Comprendre les informations données sur une personne. **A1**
- Épeler un mot et le prononcer de manière compréhensible. **A1**
- Te présenter et présenter quelqu'un (identité, personnalité). **A1**
- Échanger des informations sur ton identité. **A1**
- Comprendre un texte informatif court et simple. **A1**

Ton/ta professeur(e) te distribuera des fiches pour t'évaluer.

N'oublie pas d'utiliser :

- le lexique des couleurs (p. 29)
- le lexique de la famille (p. 29)
- les noms des pays où l'on parle anglais (p. 21, p. 29)
- les adjectifs de personnalité (p. 29)
- *be* (p. 30)
- les pronoms personnels sujets (p. 31)

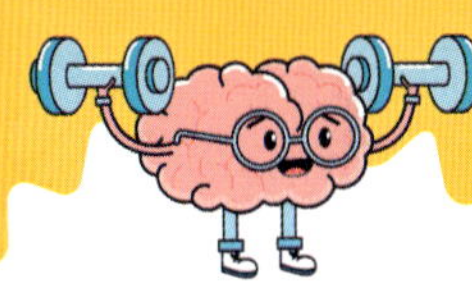

Tu veux t'améliorer ?

Rends-toi page 164 à la **Banque d'exercices** et entraîne-toi à utiliser :

- Le verbe *Be*
- Les pronoms personnels sujets
- Les mots interrogatifs
- Le lexique de l'unité

UNIT 2

Good morning

DANS CETTE UNITÉ

Tu vas découvrir

- Des écoles britanniques
- L'univers de Harry Potter
- Le 1er jour d'école des jumeaux Jones

Tu seras capable de

- Comprendre un emploi du temps
- Comprendre un règlement
- Indiquer un horaire
- Présenter des lieux de l'école
- Échanger des informations sur un règlement

Et tu vas

First Task ▸ Décider du jour préféré de la classe

Final Task ▸ Délivrer un message de bienvenue aux futurs élèves de 6e

Rhyme Time

Audio 14

MP3 20

How are you today?
I'm serious on Monday,
I'm curious on Tuesday,
I'm funny on Wednesday,
But I'm silly on Thursday,
I'm tired on Friday!
But that's OK!
Because I'm cool
on Saturday and Sunday! (x2)
Monday, Tuesday, Wednesday, (x2)
Thursday, Friday, Saturday, (x2)
Sunday!

Pupils' Interactive Activities

My Karaoke!
Entraîne-toi à chanter avec ton karaoké !

class!

School band, year 7

Re-cycle!

Remember?

Compétence
- Échanger des informations sur le matériel scolaire que l'on possède.

1. In your schoolbag

a. Listen, repeat and memorise. Audio 15

	A	B	C	D	E
1	 a **dia**ry /aɪə/	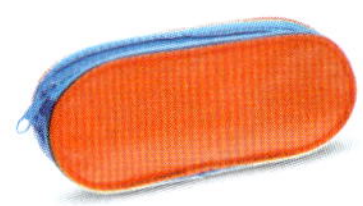 a **pen**cil case /keɪs/	 **pen**cils /e/	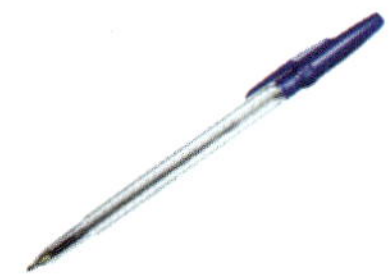 a pen /e/	 a **rub**ber /ʌ/
2	 a **high**lighter /haɪ/	 a glue stick /uː/ /ɪ/	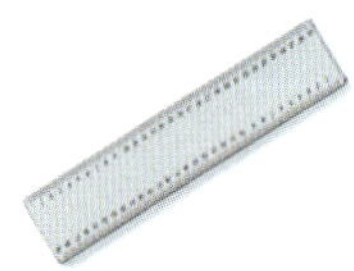 a **ru**ler /uː/	 **sciss**ors /ɪzə/	 a **cal**culator /æ/
3	 **note**books /əʊ/ /ʊ/	 books /ʊ/	 a cor**rec**tion mouse /aʊ/	 felt pens /e/	 a lunch box /ʌ/ /ɒ/

b. Look at the grid above, listen and say where the object is. Audio 16 MP3 21

Help!

On utilise l'article **the** car l'objet dont on parle est clairement défini (= celui qui est dans la case A1).

c. Copy the words in the grid. Workbook p. 20

2. The school objects battleship game

Choose three objects with your friend. Write the names of the three objects in your grid. Play with your friend: find his/her objects.

Workbook p. 21

Help!

*Your pen **is*** → nom au singulier
*Your books **are*** → nom au pluriel

3. In class!

a. Listen to two conversations and guess. Audio 17-18

Is it?...

a maths **les**son?

an **Eng**lish **les**son?

an art **les**son?

a **mu**sic **les**son?

b. Listen again. What is Peter's problem? What is Dory's problem?

Peter has got ... but he hasn't got ...

4. What's in your schoolbag?

a. Play the detective.

b. Report to the class.

Help!

a glue stick (singulier)
Ø glue sticks (pluriel)

Lesson 1 DISCOVER British schools

Compétence
- Échanger des informations sur l'environnement scolaire britannique (matières, uniformes, horaires).

1. Starting secondary school

a. Get ready to watch the video "Starting secondary school".
This is Shonny. Can you guess her age? Her country? What's different in picture 2?

b. Watch the video and check your answers. Video 02

c. Take notes in your workbook and do the activities.
Workbook p. 22

d. Use your notes to recap what you know about Shonny.
Shonny is ... / She has got ... / She is ... because ...

Help!
Aide-toi des mots que tu reconnais et des images.

2. Emily's and Tom's uniforms Audio 19

Listen to Emily and Tom. Name the different parts of their school uniforms. Workbook p. 23

3. Typical British school subjects

a. Look at the picture and guess what the slideshow is about.
The slideshow is about...

b. Watch the slideshow and check your answers. Video 03

c. Fill in the grid and recap the information.
Workbook p. 24

I like... 👍
but I don't like... 👎

4. Year 7's timetable at Halewood Academy

Spot the differences with your timetable.

They start / finish at... o'clock.

They've got ... periods in the morning.

Halewood Academy is different because ... .

Year 7 Timetable

	MONDAY	TUESDAY	WEDNESDAY	THURSDAY	FRIDAY
08:30 AM	Assembly	Registration	Registration	Registration	Registration
08:45 AM	Science *Mr Helm*	 PE *Mr O'Leary*	Science *Mr Helm*	Drama *Miss Walsh*	Woodwork *Mr Jones*
09:45 AM	Woodwork *Mr Jones*		English *Miss Darlington*	PE *Mr Rylands*	Maths *Miss Murphy*
10:45 AM	Break				
11:00 AM	English *Miss Darlington*	History *Miss Tamm*	Maths *Miss Murphy*	English *Miss Darlington*	English *Miss Darlington*
12:00 PM	Lunchtime				
1:30 PM	Dance *Mr Campbell*	Maths *Miss Murphy*	Art *Miss Carden*	French *Miss Williams*	 ICT *Miss Costello*
2:30 PM	Maths *Mr Botha*	Geography *Miss Williams*	Geography *Miss Williams*	Science *Mr Helm*	

a double period

a period

Help!

08:30 eight thirty

10:45 ten forty-five

12:00 twelve

5. The invisible timetable

MP3 22-26

Groupwork: listen and complete the timetable. Workbook p. 24

6. My favourite day

First Task

Decide on your favourite school day and explain why.

Lesson 1 GO FURTHER
Halewood or Hogwarts?

Compétences
- Identifier les lieux de l'école.
- Exprimer son opinion.

1. Halewood Academy school map

a. Look at the map and talk about the different school places in Halewood.
There is a drama hall. There are classrooms.

b. Memorise the school map for one minute. Then close your textbook.

c. Listen to the recording and say if it's right or wrong! Audio 20

1 Drama hall
2 English classroom
3 4 Science labs
5 Food technology classroom
6 ICT classroom
7 Gym
8 School library
9 Sports pitch
10 Dining hall
11 Toilets
12 Staffroom
13 14 Classrooms
15 Music classroom
16 Playground

2. Places at Hogwarts

a. Match the places with the pictures: quidditch pitch • herbology lab • potions lab • divination classroom.

b. What is your favourite school?
My favourite school is ... because there is a ... / there are ...

c. Who is your favourite character?
I like... but I don't like... Harry, Hermione, Dudley, Ron, Draco Malfoy, Snape, Sirius Black, Dumbledore, Hagrid, McGonagall, Argus Filch, Bellatrix Lestrange ...

Lesson 2 Story TIME

Compétences
- Comprendre des consignes.
- Faire des recommandations.

First day at school

1. Get ready

a. Look at the picture and say what you can.

b. Get ready to watch.

PENDANT LE VISIONNAGE, PENSE À REPÉRER
- LES VOIX (les sentiments perçus...)
- LES LIEUX de l'école
- LES MOTS connus

2. Watch the episode Video 04

a. Take notes about the twins and their school.
Workbook p. 25

b. Recap what you know.

3. Act out!

MP3 27 Workbook p. 26

a. Practise acting.

b. Memorise and act out the scene.

Pupils' Interactive Activities

Act out!
- Prépare ton rôle avec le karaoké.
- Ton/ta professeur(e) te donnera le code pour revoir l'épisode.

4. School rules! Audio 21

a. Listen and repeat. Then match the expressions with the pictures.

a. eat **chew**ing gum | **b.** talk with your friends | **c.** use your **mo**bile | **d.** run | **e.** read **com**ics | **f.** fight | **g.** be late | **h.** be **sil**ly

1 
2 
3 
4 
5 
6 
7 
8 

b. Recap the school rules.

Can you … at school / in the classroom / on the cricket pitch?

Yes, you can. / No, you can't.

Time to think

In the library, you can read books but you can't talk with your friends.

5. Recap

Write about the school rules in the different school places.

6. Sophia's tips to start school well

a. Read Sophia's message to Amelia.

b. Is Sophia's school cool or not? Workbook p. 26

So nice to meet you two!
You guys are amazing!!
Don't panic, our school is great!
Yes, Slimy and Bully are silly boys but don't be scared!
The headmaster is very strict.
Be careful in the corridors: you can't run! But don't worry, the playground is great: you can sit on the grass, and you can eat your lunch with your friends.
Now remember, you can't be late!
Your new friend, Sophia

HAVE FUN IN GROUPS

Play "I spy with my little eye"

1. Speaking Savoir épeler un mot et le mémoriser

How to play ⌛ 5 min

*** At school**

Play with 2 or more than 2 pupils!

- **Pupil A** says: "I spy with my little eye something ... *(colour)*!"
- **Pupil B** names the object.
- **Pupil C** says: "I spy with with my little eye something beginning with the letter ..."
- **Pupil D** names the object.

You win when the time is up... or when you've got 10 objects!

*** At home**

Practise on your own.

Help Yourself!

unit 2 AP

2. Listening — Identifier le sujet et prédire le contenu

→ En repérant les mots que tu connais.

→ En t'appuyant sur les photos.

★

MP3 28 Workbook p. 27

★★

MP3 29 Workbook p. 28

★★★

MP3 30 Workbook p. 29

Choose your document and go to your workbook for help.

3. Reading — Comprendre un texte court accompagné d'images

→ En repérant les mots que tu connais et en t'appuyant sur les images.

→ En identifiant le type de document.

★

★★ ★★★

Choose your activity in your workbook.

★ Workbook p. 30

★★ Workbook p. 31

★★★ Workbook p. 31

Pupils' Interactive Activities

Entraîne-toi avec les exercices interactifs.

Memorise the words!

1 Schoolbag

Play with your partner. Do it as fast as you can!
- **Pupil A** points at an object in his/her schoolbag.
- **Pupil B** names it in English.

2 Uniforms

Spelling game! **Pupil A** points to an item on page 47 and **pupil B** spells it.

B-L-A-Z-E-R
"blazer!"

3 School subjects

Choose a subject and play hangman with your classmates!

Practise!

A La prononciation du pluriel

Contrairement au français, la terminaison –s du pluriel des noms se prononce en anglais. Il existe trois prononciations possibles :

/ɪz/ → pencil cases, buses
/z/ → pens
/s/ → books

1. Écoute et répète les mots suivants. Place ta main sur ta gorge et sens si tes cordes vocales vibrent ou non. Qu'en déduis-tu ? Audio 22 MP3 31

keys / pencil cases / books / glue sticks / pens / skirts / trousers / rulers / shoes / shirts / school badges / rubbers / school places / socks

2. Écoute. Quel est l'intrus ? Audio 23 MP3 32

a. *names - pens - addresses*
b. *books - twins - shirts*
c. *badges - brothers - oranges*

B La prononciation de la lettre « *u* »

En anglais, il faut faire attention à la relation « graphie-phonie » : une même lettre à l'écrit (« **graphie** ») n'a pas toujours le même son à l'oral (« **phonie** »).

Graphie	Phonie
uniform	/ˈjuːnɪfɔːm/
rubber	/ˈrʌbə/
ruler	/ˈruːlə/
Thursday	/ˈθɜːzdeɪ/

Écoute et classe des mots avec la lettre « u » dans ton workbook. Audio 24 MP3 33 Workbook p. 32

C La prononciation de *Can* et *Can't*

L'auxiliaire *can* a deux prononciations selon sa place dans la phrase.

Can		Can't
/kæn/	/kən/	/kɑːnt/
• Dans les questions : *"Can I look at the costumes?"* • Dans les réponses brèves : *"Yes, you can."*	• À la forme affirmative : *"They can show you the school later."*	• À la forme négative : *"Remember, you can't touch anything!"*

Écoute, répète et entraîne-toi ! Audio 25 MP3 34

Can I look at the costumes? / Of course you **can**! / You **can't** teleport at school! / You **can't** use *your* powers here. / **Can** you do sports at lunch time? / You **can** look at the costumes.

Days of the week MP3 35

Monday	Tuesday	Wednesday	Thursday	Friday	Saturday
/ʌ/	/tjuːz/	/ˈwenzdeɪ/	/θɜːz/	/fraɪ/	/æ/
					Sunday /ʌ/

Your schoolbag MP3 36

a **ru**ler /uː/
a **rub**ber /ʌ/
a glue stick /uː/ /ɪ/
a **note**book /əʊ/ /ʊ/
a pen /e/
scissors /ˈsɪzəz/
a book /ʊ/
a **pen**cil case /ˈpensl keɪs/
a **high**lighter /aɪ/
a **cal**culator /æ/
a cor**rec**tion mouse /ʃən/ /aʊ/
felt pens /e/
a lunch box /lʌntʃ/
a **dia**ry /aɪə/
a **time**table /aɪ/ /eɪ/

School uniforms MP3 37

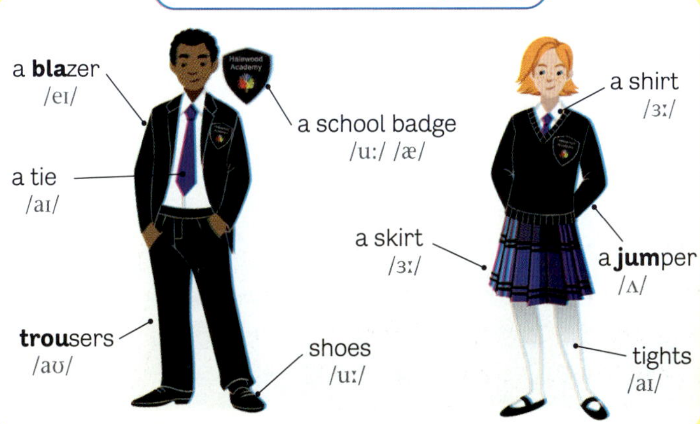

School subjects MP3 38

English /ɪŋ/
maths /mæθs/
ge**og**raphy /dʒɪ/
history /ˈhɪstəri/
science /aɪ/
ICT /aɪ siː tiː/
PE /piː iː/
French /e/
music /juː/
art /ɑː/
De**sign** & Tech**nol**ogy (D&T) /aɪn/

School places MP3 39

the **class**room /ɑː/
the gym /ɪ/
the **sci**ence lab /aɪ/ /æ/
the **play**ground /eɪ/ /aʊ/
the head's **of**fice /e/ /ɒ/
the **li**brary /aɪ/
sports fields /ɔː/ /iː/
the **di**ning hall /aɪ/

PE kit / Sports uniform MP3 40

Homework Workbook p. 34-36
Des exercices supplémentaires pour t'entraîner.

→ Pour exprimer ce que l'on possède

Have got

Forme affirmative

Forme pleine
I **have got**
you **have got**
he/she/it **has got**
we/you/they **have got**

Forme contractée
I'**ve got**
you'**ve got**
he/she/it'**s got**
we/you/they'**ve got**

À la 3e personne du singulier, *have* devient *has*.

Forme négative

I **haven't got**
you **haven't got**
he/she/it **hasn't got**
we/you/they **haven't got**

À la forme négative, on utilise plutôt la forme contractée.

He's got blue trousers.
He hasn't got a blazer.

Dans les questions, on inverse *have* avec le sujet.

Forme interrogative

Have I **got... ?**
Have you **got... ?**
Has he/she/it **got... ?**
Have we/you/they **got... ?**

Réponses brèves

Affirmatives (Yes, ...)	Négatives (No, ...)
I **have**.	I **haven't**.
You **have**.	You **haven't**.
He/she/it **has**.	He/she/it **hasn't**.
We/you/they **have**.	We/you/they **haven't**.

1 Devine ce que ton/ta professeur(e) a dans son sac ! Pose-lui la question.
Have you got a pencil case / a lunch box?

2 Reconstruis les questions, puis réponds-y.
a. *mobile / a / you / Have / got / ?*
b. *Monday / Have / music / you / on / lesson / got / a / ?*
c. *friend / got / calculator / Has / your / a / ?*
d. *Shonny / tie / a / Has / got / ?*
e. *bedroom / she / got / a / flag / in / Has / her / ?*
f. *labs / got / Hogwarts / they / at / Have / ?*
g. *a / school / got / Have / rugby / at / Oliver and Amelia / pitch / ?*

3 Décris l'uniforme des élèves de Hogwarts.
Ron has got... but he hasn't got...

→ Pour indiquer ou demander ce qui est permis ou non

Can

Ce qui est possible, car autorisé, s'énonce avec *can*.

You can read comics in the school library.

(= C'est autorisé.)

Can't

Ce qui est impossible, car interdit, s'énonce avec *can't*.

You can't run in the library.

(= Ce n'est pas autorisé.)

La négation de *can* (*cannot*) apparaît le plus souvent sous sa forme contractée *can't*.

Can I + BV?

Pour demander l'autorisation, on pose la question : *"Can I* + BV*?"*

Can I open the window, please?

L'action autorisée ou interdite s'exprime avec la base verbale *(read, run...)*.

4 Complète avec *can* ou *can't* le règlement affiché en classe.

a. *You ... sit next to your friend but you ... chat.*

b. *You ... have a snack in your bag but you ... eat it in class.*

c. *You ... use your mobile but you ... use your school tablet computer.*

5 Mr et Mrs Jones ont affiché un rappel pour leurs enfants sur la porte d'entrée. Complète-le avec *can* ou *can't*.

You ... use your powers at home
but you ... use them at school.
You ... teleport to school but
you ... teleport for shopping.
You ... tell your friends about
your powers!

6 Explique la signification des panneaux que tu vois au musée. Action: *Look / Touch / Use*

a. b. c. d.

7 Explique les règles ci-dessous.

a. Football: *You ... kick the ball with your foot, but you ... touch it with your hand. You ... hit the ball with your head.*

b. Tennis: *You ...*

8 En classe, tu dois demander la permission pour certaines choses. Que diras-tu dans ces situations ?

a. b. c. d.

Final Task

Domaine 2 Socle

Deliver a welcome message to the new pupils

Ton projet

Ton collège souhaite diffuser sur son blog un message vidéo de bienvenue à destination des élèves qui entreront en 6e l'an prochain. L'objectif est de rassurer les futurs élèves en leur présentant de manière simple la vie au collège.
Suis les étapes ci-dessous pour préparer ton message.

Les étapes à suivre

STEP 1
You're the guide!
Tu es le guide, donc commence par te présenter brièvement.

STEP 2
School places & rules
Présente deux lieux et quelques règles de ton collège (ex.: *In the... you can/can't ...*)

STEP 3
A new timetable!
Donne quelques informations sur l'emploi du temps :
- les horaires de début et fin de journée
- le nombre de cours par jour
- les matières étudiées

STEP 4
And now, record yourself!
Enregistre ton message en vidéo ou présente-le à la classe.

A positive message.
Sois positif(ve) et rassurant(e) ! Par exemple : *Your new school is a great school! It's fun!*

I BET YOU CAN!

MAINTENANT, TU ES CAPABLE DE :

- Comprendre des consignes. A1
- Comprendre des mots et des expressions sur un environnement scolaire. A1
- Décrire ton environnement scolaire (emploi du temps, lieu, matériel…). A1
- Échanger des informations sur l'école (horaire, matériel, disciplines…). A1
- Comprendre un règlement. A1
- Isoler des informations dans un court texte. A1
- Nommer des objets et savoir les écrire. A1

Ton/ta professeur(e) te distribuera des fiches pour t'évaluer.

N'oublie pas d'utiliser :

- le lexique de l'emploi du temps : matières scolaires, horaires (p.47)
- les lieux de l'école (p.47)
- des actions permises ou non à l'école (p.43)
- *have got* (p.48)
- *can* et *can't* (p.49)
- les expressions pour émettre une opinion favorable (*It's fun*, etc.) (p.43)

Tu veux t'améliorer ?

Rends-toi page 165 à la **Banque d'exercices** et entraîne-toi à utiliser :

- *Have got*
- *Can / Can't*
- Le lexique de l'unité

UNIT 3

This is my family

DANS CETTE UNITÉ

Tu vas découvrir

- La famille royale britannique
- L'univers des films *Hotel Transylvania*
- D'autres membres très spéciaux de la famille Jones !

Tu seras capable de

- Lire et comprendre un court texte sur la famille
- Lire et comprendre une description physique
- Présenter une famille
- Exprimer tes goûts et tes talents
- Dialoguer sur ta famille, tes goûts et tes talents

Et tu vas

First Task ▸ Écrire une carte postale

Final Task ▸ Créer une affiche pour le concours de “la plus incroyable des super familles”

Rhyme Time

Audio 26

MP3 41

What about my family?

My father's got a mother, she's my grandmother,
My mother's got a father, he's my grandfather,
My parents have a daughter, she's my sister,
She's really cool and funny and I love her!
Family, what about my family?
Fa-fa-fa-family, what about my family? (x2)
My uncle's got a brother, he's my father,
My aunty's got a sister, she's my mother,
They also have a son, his name is Connor,
He's my cousin and he's good at soccer!
Family, what about my family?
Fa-fa-fa-family, what about my family? (x2)

Pupils' Interactive Activities

My Karaoke!
Entraîne-toi à chanter avec ton karaoké !

ily!

“Hotel Transylvania 3”, an animated film

Re-cycle!

Remember?

Compétences
- Échanger des informations sur les liens de parenté.
- Nommer quelques animaux domestiques.

1. A famous family

a. Read the texts. Make a list of all the family vocabulary. Audio 27-28

December 2020

Do you know me? **I'm William.**
My grandmother is the Queen and my grandfather is a prince, Prince Philip.
I've got one brother, Harry, so I am Archie's uncle.
My father is Prince Charles. My mother, Diana, died in 1997 in an accident.
My stepmother is Camilla.

I'm Kate. I'm William's wife.
We've got two sons, George and Louis, and a daughter, Charlotte.
We love children!
My parents are Carol and Michael Middleton. I've got a sister, Pippa, and a brother, James.
They're great!

b. Listen to all the family vocabulary. Check your list. What is the new word in the recording? Audio 29

c. Use the family vocabulary to complete Peter's family tree. Workbook p. 37

d. Complete the royal family tree with the names of the family members. Workbook p. 38

2. Queen Elizabeth's family

Interact with your friend to identify Harry, Camilla, Kate, Anne, Meghan and William.

Who is Anne?

She is the Queen's daughter. She is Charles's sister.

Time to think

The Queen is William's grandmother.
Le lien de parenté entre William et la Reine est exprimé par « 's ». L'ordre des mots est inversé par rapport au français (la grand-mère de William).

3. The Royals love animals!

Audio 30

a. Listen and repeat the names of the animals.

Help!

one cat → two cats
Attention ! *one mouse → two mice*
one goldfish → two goldfish

b. What animals have they got?

c. Find out about your classmate's pets.

Have you got ...?

Yes, I have. / No, I haven't.

Lesson 1 DISCOVER
A legendary family

Compétences
- Comprendre la description physique d'un personnage.
- Écrire une courte description.

1. A strange family

a. Look at the family tree, listen to the texts and "read along". Audio 31

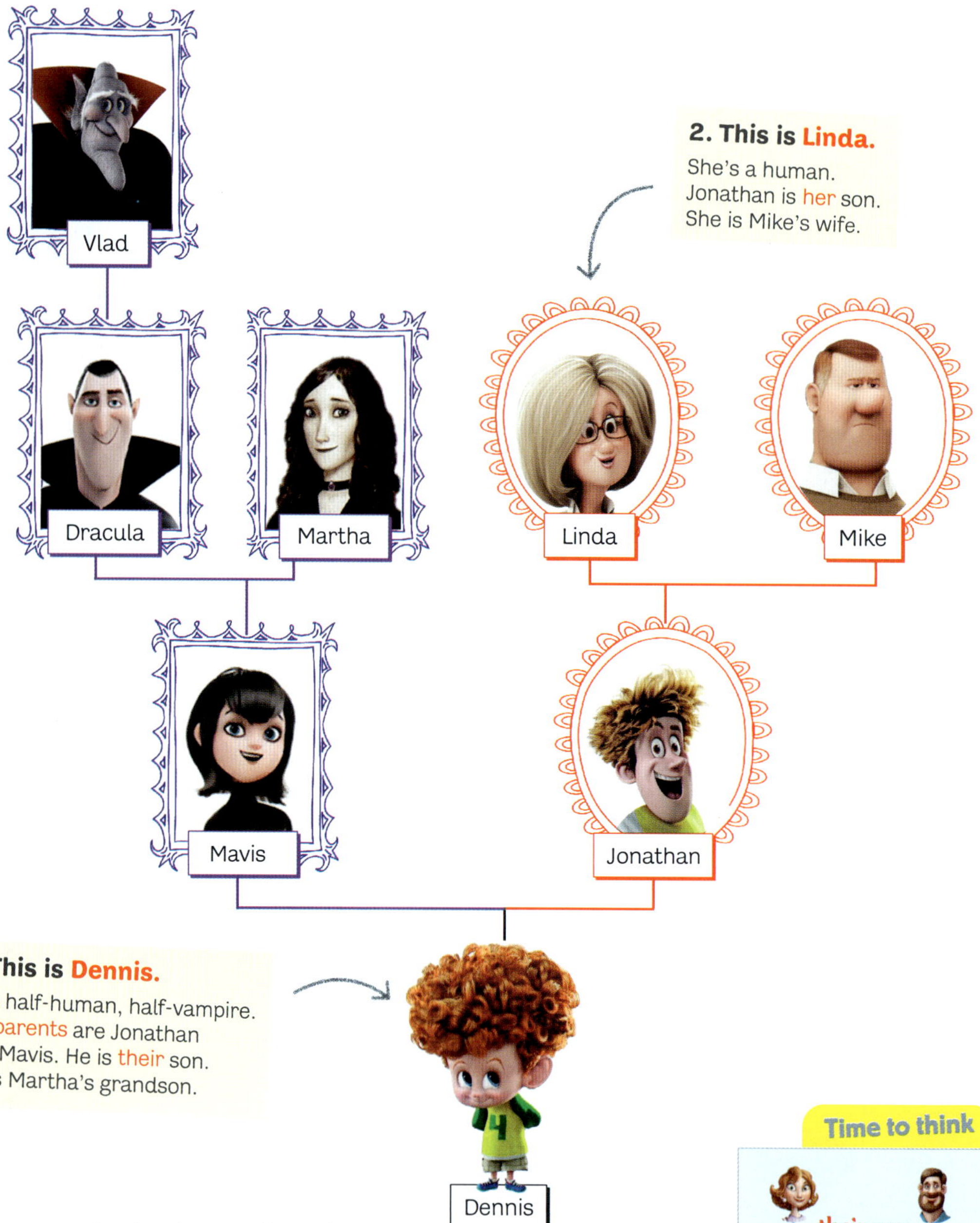

1. This is Vlad.
He's a very old vampire.
Dracula is his son.
He is Mavis's grandfather.

2. This is Linda.
She's a human.
Jonathan is her son.
She is Mike's wife.

3. This is Dennis.
He's half-human, half-vampire.
His parents are Jonathan and Mavis. He is their son.
He is Martha's grandson.

b. Use the model to recap the family relationships.
Example: *Mavis has got a son. His name is Dennis. Dennis is Mavis's son.*

Time to think

2. A family portrait

a. Listen to the descriptions as you read. Audio 32-33

FRANK

He's got a long square face and short black hair. He's got a small nose, small ears and a big smile but he is ugly. He's very tall and very big. His feet are very big. He's got a white and blue shirt, a red tie and a blue suit: a blue blazer and blue trousers.

Mavis

She's not very tall and she's slim. She's got a round face, a small nose and big blue eyes. She's got straight black hair. She's got a lovely smile and she's got fangs because she's a vampire. She's got a black dress, red and black tights and red trainers.

b. Pick out the words related to physical descriptions and complete the drawings in your workbook. Workbook p. 39

c. Read the descriptions of Dennis and Murray. Match the texts and the pictures. Workbook p. 40

3. Trouble at the hotel

Vlad **hasn't got** his phone and Dennis **hasn't got** his teddy bear.

a. Listen to the two conversations and find who has got the phone and the teddy bear. Audio 34-35 Workbook p. 40

b. Play the "Who's who?" game with the whole family of *Hotel Transylvania 2*. Workbook p. 40

Help!

a square face / small ears

Dans le groupe nominal, l'adjectif se place avant le nom. Il est invariable.

4. Holiday postcard

First Task

You are on a school trip and you are with a host family. Write a postcard about your host family (names, family relationships, physical descriptions).

Lesson 1 GO FURTHER
Families in the Arts

Compétences
- Identifier la nature d'un document.
- Décrire un personnage.

1. Fantastic Mr Fox

a. Look carefully at all the elements which compose this document and identify it.

b. Where can you find document 1 and document 2 (right page) ?

An American film (2009) adapted from Roald Dahl's novel (1970)

2. The Gravenor family

a. Describe the scene. What can you imagine about this family?

b. Do you think some elements look strange? Which ones?

Thomas Gainsborough is one of the greatest British painters of the 18th century.
He made the portrait of the Gravenor family: John and Ann, the parents, and their two daughters: Elizabeth and Ann.

The Gravenor Family, (1754), by Thomas Gainsborough

Lesson 2 Story TIME

Compétence
- Échanger des informations sur ce que l'on sait faire et sur ses goûts.

A mysterious family

1. Get ready

Look at the title of the episode and at the picture. Say what you can.

2. Watch the episode

Video 05

a. Go to your workbook and take notes on the family members. Workbook p. 42

b. Recap what you know about the Joneses and their friends.
Why are they a super family?

3. Act out!

MP3 42 Workbook p. 43

a. Practise acting.

b. Memorise and act out the scene.

Help!

*I **can** run but I **can't** fly.*

- **I can + BV**
  = ce que je sais faire, ce dont je suis capable.
- **I can't + BV**
  = ce que je ne sais pas faire, ce dont je ne suis pas capable.

Pupils' Interactive Activities

Act out!
- Prépare ton rôle avec le karaoké.
- Ton/ta professeur(e) te donnera le code pour revoir l'épisode.

4. Are you sporty or artistic?

a. Look at the pictures. Listen, repeat and memorise. Audio 36

b. Take the test. Say what you can / can't do. Then give your friend the test. Workbook p. 44

dance

play an instrument

ride a bike

draw

climb
/ˈklaɪm/

swim

play football

do gymnastics

Can you swim?

Yes, I can. / No, I can't.

5. Are you the indoor type or the outdoor type?

a. Classify the activities according to their category. MP3 43 Workbook p. 44
Then write about your profile. Workbook p. 45

I like surfing the web and I like riding a bike but I don't like playing rugby.

b. Ask your friend five questions about his/her profile.

Time to think

He likes cooking.
❤ Ce que l'on aime faire :
sujet + like/likes + V-ing

She doesn't like playing video games.
❤ Ce que l'on n'aime pas faire :
Sujet + don't/doesn't like + V-ing

play video games

listen to music

cook

watch TV

go for a bike ride

play outside

go shopping

meet friends outside

Do you like...?

Yes, I do. / No, I don't.

6. The Super Profiles challenges.

Go to your workbook and follow the challenges to write your superhero profile. Workbook p. 45

HAVE FUN IN GROUPS

Play “Happy Families”

1. Speaking — Dialoguer sur un sujet familier (famille, liens de parenté)

How to play ⧗ 10 min

- From 2 to 4 players
- The goal is to collect whole families. The winner is the player with the most families.

* Give 5 cards to each player. The rest of the cards form a stock.

* Ask a player for a specific card from a family: *“Please, can I have the mother in the Windsor family?”*

- If the player does not have the card, he/she says ***“Pick a card!”***
- If the player picks the right card, he/she says ***“Lucky dip!”*** and plays again.
- As soon as a player collects a set of 5 cards of the same family, he/she must say ***“Happy family!”***

Help Yourself!

2. Listening — Isoler des informations simples dans un message

→ En prenant appui sur le contexte et les visuels et en formulant des hypothèses.
→ En repérant les champs lexicaux.

★

MP3 45 Workbook p. 46

★★

MP3 46 Workbook p. 46

★★★

MP4 47 Workbook p. 47

Choose your document and go to your workbook for help.

3. Writing — Rédiger un texte guidé sur un personnage imaginaire

→ En étoffant une description de personnage à l'aide d'adjectifs.
→ En utilisant des mots de liaison simples (*and*, *but*...).

Choose your character and your activity in your workbook.

★ Workbook p. 48

★★ Workbook p. 49

★★★ Workbook p. 49

Language Lab Words & Sounds

Pupils' Interactive Activities

Entraîne-toi avec les exercices interactifs.

Memorise the words!

1 Family members

Imagine you're a member of the Royal family: explain who the other members are for you.

Hi! I'm William's brother and the Queen is my grandmother, who am I?

You're Harry!

2 Physical description

Pictionary game!

Pupil A draws a face or a person.

Pupil B: *"She's got a small nose!".*

3 Find out your teacher's secret talents.

Ask questions about what he/she can do.

Pupil: *"Miss/Sir, can you sing?"*

Teacher: *"Yes, I can. / No, I can't."*

Practise!

A La prononciation de la lettre « o »

La lettre « o » peut se prononcer de plusieurs façons.

Graphie	Phonie
mother	/'mʌðər/
nose	/nəʊz/
short	/ʃɔːt/
stop	/stɒp/

Listen and repeat. Audio 37 MP3 48

mother – brother – son – nose – short – video – horse – teleport – stop – transform – monsters – protect

B La prononciation du génitif

Comment prononcer la marque du génitif correctement ? Souviens-toi de la règle de prononciation des pluriels vue dans l'unité 2 (p. 46). C'est la même règle qui s'applique pour prononcer « 's » !

*Charlotte**'s** brother* /s/

*George**'s** sister* /ɪz/

*William**'s** children* /z/

Read, listen and check. Audio 38 MP3 49

George's sister – Harry's father – The Queen's hat – Camilla's husband – Princess Anne's mother - Charles's family – The princess's toys – The prince's schoolbag

C L'intonation des questions fermées

Lorsque tu peux répondre à une question uniquement par oui ou par non, on parle de questions fermées. On les appelle les « YES/NO questions » en anglais. Ces questions portent une intonation montante sur le dernier mot accentué.

Listen, repeat and practise! Audio 39 MP3 50

Can they **te**leport?

Have they got powers?

Can they fly?

Do you play an **in**strument?

Faces MP3 51

a **fun**ny face /ʌ/ /eɪ/

a square face /eə/

a round face /aʊ/

a small nose /ɔː/ /əʊ/

a big nose /ɪ/

short hair /ɔː/ /heə/

long hair /ɒŋ/

straight hair /eɪ/

curly hair /ɜː/

red hair /e/

a big smile /ɪ/

a **love**ly smile /ʌ/ /aɪ/

big blue eyes /ɪ/ /uː//aɪ/

small green eyes /ɔː/ /iː/

Activities MP3 52

play an **in**strument /eɪ/ /ʊ/

play **vid**eo games /eɪ/ /əʊ//eɪ/

play **out**side /eɪ/ /aɪ/

cook /ʊ/

draw /ɔː/

paint /eɪ/

do gym**nas**tics /dʒɪm//æ/

meet friends /miːt frendz/

watch TV /ɒ/ /tiːviː/

ride a bike /aɪ/ /aɪ/

ride a horse /aɪ/ /ɔː/

dance /ɑː/

listen to **mu**sic /ɪ/ /juː/

Adjectives MP3 53

tall ≠ small /ɔː/ /ɔː/

big ≠ slim /ɪ/ /ɪ/

cute ≠ **ug**ly /juː/ /ʌ/

strong /ɒ/

fast ≠ slow /ɑː/ /əʊ/

A family MP3 54

grandparents

an aunt /ɑː/

an **un**cle /ʌ/

a **hus**band /ʌ/

a wife /aɪ/

a son /ʌ/

a **daugh**ter /ɔː/

A stepfamily

a **step**mother /ʌ/

stepsisters /ɪ/

The human body MP3 55

the head /hed/

an arm /ɑː/

a hand /æ/

a leg /e/

feet /iː/

Homework Workbook p. 52-55
Des exercices supplémentaires pour t'entraîner.

→ Pour exprimer un lien de parenté ou la possession

Le génitif

- **Le possesseur est placé avant le nom.**

Il est relié à l'objet ou à la personne qu'il définit par « **'s** » : c'est la marque du génitif.

It's a cat.

It's Tim's cat.

Tim is Sarah's brother.

- **Le lien est uniquement l'apostrophe.**

My parent**s'** dog → possesseur = nom au pluriel terminé en -s
Charles**'s** dog → possesseur = nom propre terminé en -s

Les déterminants possessifs

*The Queen has got three dogs: **her** dogs are corgis.*
*Prince Charles has got a dog too: **his** dog is a labrador.*

- Si le possesseur est masculin → **his**
- Si le possesseur est féminin → **her**
- S'il y a plusieurs possesseurs (pluriel) : → **their**

1 Do you like their hats?

a.

I like... / I don't like...

b.

c.

2 His or her?

a. – This is Paul's father, Max.
– I see! Max is ... father.

b. – Yes and this is Paul's mother, Helen.
– I see, Helen is ... mother.

c. – Who is Cindy? Jane's sister?
– Yes, it's ... sister. And Tim is ... brother.

3 Complete with *my*, *your*, *his* or *her*. **Who is it?**

"Hello! (...) name is ? . (...) brother has got three children. (...) wife is beautiful. She's got a sister: (...) name is Pippa. I have two children, (...) son's name is Archie. What about you? What's (...) name?"

→ Pour parler de ce que quelqu'un est capable de faire ou non

Can

Pour dire ce qu'on est **capable** de faire, on utilise l'auxiliaire ***can***.

→ **CAN + base verbale** (action)

Can't

Pour dire ce qu'on n'est **pas capable** de faire, on utilise la forme négative.

→ **CAN'T + base verbale** (action)

*Amelia's grandfather **can** run very fast, but he **can't** cook.*

5 What can or can't they do?

a. James isn't very sporty: he ... a bike.

b. Jenny is an artist: she ... .

c. Mary is wonderful, she ... delicious lasagna.

d. I love music and I ... the piano but I ... very well.

6 What are their talents?

a. My sister / play tennis

b. My teacher / speak English

c. My friend / speak Italian

d. Usain Bolt / run fast

→ Pour parler de ses goûts ou de ceux de quelqu'un

Like

À la forme affirmative

→ Like + nom / V-ing

→ Likes + nom / V-ing (3e pers. du singulier)

I like sports. My sister likes listening to music.

À la forme négative

→ Don't like + nom / V-ing

→ Doesn't like + nom / V-ing (3e pers. du singulier)

I don't like tennis.
My sister doesn't like video games.

À la forme interrogative

→ Do + Sujet + like + nom / V-ing

→ Does + sujet 3e personne + like + nom / V-ing

Do you like curry?
Does your Dad like cooking?

7 Complete with the correct form of *like*.

a. (You / like) ... the film Frozen? (Your friend/like) ... it?

b. Elsa is the Snow Queen. She ... Olaf but she ... Bruni.
Her sister, Anna, ... horse-riding but she ... cold weather.

c. I ... Olaf, he is funny but I ... Prince Hans, he is cruel!

8 Read what Mavis and Jonathan. Who do/don't they like?

Final Task

Domaine 2 Socle

Create a poster and win the Super Family Competition

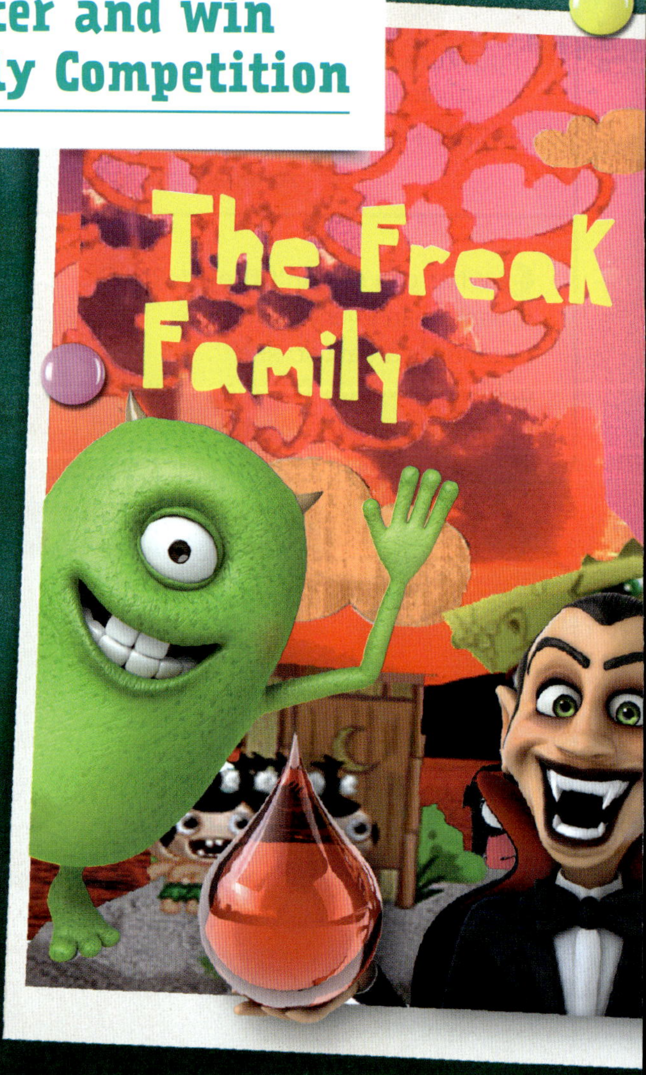

Ton projet

Tu as de l'imagination ! Remporte le concours organisé par ton/ta professeur(e) en inventant une « super famille » !
Les trois affiches préférées seront publiées sur le blog de ton collège ou affichées dans ton collège.

Les étapes à suivre

STEP 1
Identity
Invente une identité à ta famille. Définis à quelle catégorie ils/elles appartiennent *(vampire, werewolf, aliens, superhero...)*.

STEP 2
Description
À quoi ressemblent-ils ? Ont-ils l'air drôle, terrifiant, sympathique... ?

STEP 3
Personality & profiles
Décris leur personnalité, trouve au moins deux qualités.
À partir de ces qualités, imagine ce que cette personne aime ou pas, ce qu'elle est capable de faire ou non.

STEP 4
Make a super poster
Pour créer ton poster : cherche des visuels ou dessine ta super famille.

STEP 5
And now, vote!
Tu as trois points à ta disposition. Choisis à quels posters tu les attribues et justifie ton choix d'une phrase.

I BET YOU CAN!

MAINTENANT, TU ES CAPABLE DE :

- Comprendre des informations données sur une personne et sur une famille. A1
- Décrire une personne. A1
- Parler de goûts et d'habitudes à propos de soi ou d'un autre. A1
- Dialoguer sur un sujet familier (liens de parenté, goûts et talents, animaux domestiques). A1
- Isoler des informations simples dans la description d'une famille et/ou d'une personne. A1
- Identifier le sujet d'une conversation. A2

Ton/ta professeur(e) te distribuera des fiches pour t'évaluer.

N'oublie pas d'utiliser :

- le lexique de :
  - la famille (p. 65)
  - la description physique (p. 65)
  - les activités et les talents (p. 65)
- *have got* (p. 48)
- *can* et *can't* (p. 67)
- *like + V-ing / don't like* (p. 67)

Tu veux t'améliorer ?

Rends-toi page 166 à la **Banque d'exercices** et entraîne-toi à utiliser :

- Le génitif
- *Can / can't*
- *Like*
- Le lexique de l'unité

UNIT 4

Welcome to my

DANS CETTE UNITÉ

Tu vas découvrir

- Des maisons britanniques et américaines
- Quelques secrets sur les habitudes des Jones

Tu seras capable de

- Comprendre la description d'une maison
- Comprendre la routine de quelqu'un
- Parler de ta maison
- Situer un objet dans l'espace
- Parler de tes habitudes ou de celles d'une autre personne
- Échanger des informations sur ton environnement
- Dialoguer sur ta routine quotidienne

Et tu vas

First Task ▸ Imaginer une maison de star

Final Task ▸ Comparer vos habitudes avec ton(ta) correspondant(e) avant un échange scolaire

Rhyme Time

Audio 40

MP3 56

My crazy house

I've got a house, just a crazy house!
There's a chicken in the kitchen,
And a panda on the sofa!
There's a hamster on my computer,
And a turtle on the table!
I've got a house, just a crazy house! (x 2)
There's a rabbit on the carpet,
An alligator on the radiator,
There's a bear, sat on a chair,
And a monkey's got the key!
I've got a house, just a crazy house! (x 4)

Pupils' Interactive Activities

My Karaoke!
Entraîne-toi à chanter avec ton karaoké !

house!

Victorian houses in London

Re-cycle!

Remember?

Compétences
- Comprendre la description d'une maison.
- Échanger des informations sur son environnement.

1. Jazzy's gigantic house

a. Watch the video. Can you name the rooms in Jazzy's house? Video 06

b. What do you think of her house?

c. Label the pictures in your workbook. Workbook p. 56

Houston, Texas
(The United States of America)

2. More rooms and places in Jazzy's house!

a. Jazzy loves sending text messages. Read the messages to her friends.

b. Listen, repeat and memorise. Audio 41

c. Close your textbook. Go to your workbook and do the exercises. Workbook p. 57

Look! This is my front garden!

Here is the study!

That's the entrance door…

The backgarden and the swimming pool!

3. Your new home

a. Listen, repeat and point at the objects in the two rooms. Then memorise them. Audio 42

b. Talk about your new home.

The kitchen.
It's nice:
there is... / there are...

Help!
a kettle
an oven

Look at the bedroom!
There is... / there are...

4. In your friend's house

a. Ask your friend about his / her kitchen and bedroom.

b. Say what is in your friend's kitchen/bedroom.

In my friend's kitchen/bedroom, there is/isn't ... / there are/aren't ...

Is there a ... in your ... ?
Are there ... in your ... ?

Yes, there is. / No, there isn't.
Yes, there are. / No, there aren't.

Lesson 1 DISCOVER
A British home

Compétences
- Situer un objet dans l'espace.
- Décrire sa maison.
- Échanger des informations sur son environnement.

1. Wallace and Gromit's living room

Wallace and Gromit: A Grand Day Out, a film by Nick Park

Help!

- in
- on
- under
- behind
- between
- in front of
- next to

a. Listen and point at the objects. Audio 43

b. Label the picture in your workbook. Workbook p. 58

c. Describe Wallace and Gromit's living room in your workbook. Listen and check. Workbook p. 59

2. Spot the differences

a. Work in pairs: in the workbook, pupil A looks at the picture on p. 59, pupil B looks at the picture on p. 60. Workbook p. 59-60

b. Recap the differences between the two pictures.
In picture A, the schoolbag is under the bed.
In picture B, the schoolbag is next to the desk.

3. A house swap for the holidays!

a. Find the house corresponding to the following indications.

- Modern house
- 3 bedrooms
- Large living room
- Small garden
- No garage

The Briggs | *The Smarts* | *The Williams*

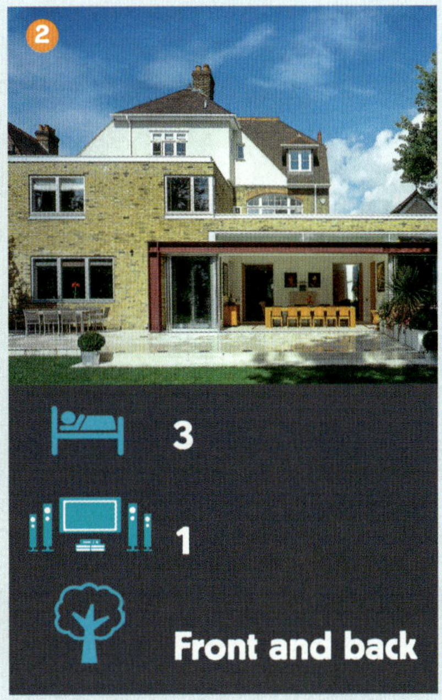

b. Three families are looking for a house to swap for their holidays. Listen to them and take notes.
Audio 44 Workbook p. 60

c. Who is ready to swap with who?

4. Home, sweet home!

The family loves their house. They write a short email to their friends to describe their new holiday home. Workbook p. 61

5. My celebrity house!

First Task

You're a new celebrity.
Describe your house,
draw the plan and justify the eccentricities!

Example: *My house is fantastic.*
There is a pool in the living room because ... !

An eco-friendly house in Australia

Lesson 1 GO FURTHER
Houses of power and poetry

Compétence
- Identifier des repères culturels et géographiques.

1. Who lives in these houses?

The Queen • The President of the United States of America • The British Prime Minister

A

The White House

B

10, Downing Street

C

Buckingham Palace

2. A cottage

a. This cottage is near Galway. Is it in England, Scotland or Ireland? Have a look at the map at the beginning of your textbook.
b. Is it the home of a rich man or a farmer or an aristocrat?
c. Do you think the interior is modern, comfortable and spacious?

3. Houses in a famous street

a. Where is this street?
b. Look at the street sculpture and guess why this street is famous. For help, look at p. 158.

Lesson 2 Story TIME

Compétences
- Comprendre une routine.
- Parler de ses habitudes.
- Dialoguer sur les routines.

A day at the Joneses'

1. Get ready

a. Talk about your habits.

never
sometimes
often
always

do the cooking

put the shopping away

do the cleaning

take the pet out

b. Look at the title of the episode and at the picture and say what you can.

2. Watch the episode Video 07

a. Take notes on what the Joneses do on weekends. Workbook p. 61

b. Recap what you know.

3. Act out! MP3 57

a. Practise acting. Workbook p. 62

b. Memorise and act out the scene.

Pupils' Interactive Activities

Act out!
- Prépare ton rôle avec le karaoké.
- Ton/ta professeur(e) te donnera le code pour revoir l'épisode.

4. The Magic Routine Maker

TEACHER'S SLIDES

a. Listen, repeat and memorise. Audio 45

b. Classify the activities into two categories: "Lucky you" or "Poor You". Workbook p. 63

c. Listen to people reading their tickets and react with: "Lucky you!" or "Poor you!" Audio 46

d. Write "Lucky you!" and "Poor you!" tickets.

5. A lucky or an unlucky routine?

Read the tickets from the Magic Routine Maker. Is it a "lucky routine" or an "unlucky routine"? Workbook p. 63

6. Your lucky routine

a. Your friend got a ticket from the Magic Routine Maker. Ask your friend questions and take notes.

Do you sometimes get up late?

Yes, I do.

No, I don't. I never get up late.

Sorry, I haven't got it on my ticket!

b. Is your friend lucky or unlucky? Use your notes to recap.

Peter is lucky: he never tidies his room and he always has fun outside.

Time to think

Amelia often takes Morph out.
Does she do the shopping?
No, she doesn't and she doesn't hoover.

HAVE FUN IN GROUPS

Play "Let's enter the house"

1. Speaking Parler de ses habitudes

How to play ⌛ 10 min

* Let's enter the house! Roll the dice and follow the arrows. Say what you see, what you do or don't do in each room you enter.
* To win points make sentences.
  - ★ *There is / there are* ... + object(s) = **1 point**
  - ★★ *I don't* + verb = **2 points**
  - ★★★ *I* + adverb + verb = **3 points**

  Example: *I often read in the garden.*

Help!

Nouns
cupboard - mirror - kettle - bed - table - chair - sofa - lamp - car - books - plants - TV - fireplace

Verbs
play - break - eat - open

Help Yourself!

unit 4 AP

2. Listening Reconstruire du sens à partir d'éléments significatifs

→ En s'appuyant sur les indices visuels pour anticiper sur le contenu.
→ En écoutant de manière globale pour confirmer des hypothèses.
→ En repérant des mots-clés en fonction d'une thématique définie.

Choose your activity and go to your workbook.

★

MP3 58 Workbook p. 64

★★

MP3 59 Workbook p. 65

★★★

MP3 60 Workbook p. 65

3. Speaking Mobiliser ses acquis langagiers pour produire un message oral

→ En listant et en organisant les éléments dont tu as besoin.
→ En structurant ton énoncé avec des adverbes de fréquence et des mots de liaison.

Leave a voice message for Super Mary. Use what you know about the families from activity 2 (above).
- Tell her the family's new habits.
- Thank her for her help.

Choose your activity in your workbook.

★ Workbook p. 66

★★ Workbook p. 67

★★★ Workbook p. 67

Super Mary fights bad habits!

Language Lab *Words & Sounds*

Pupils' Interactive Activities
Entraîne-toi avec les exercices interactifs.

Memorise the words!

1 Rooms and objects

Pupil A names an object.
Pupil B says where it is.

2 Where is it?

Use prepositions to locate objects and pupils in the classroom.

3 Your routine

Speak about your routine in 30 seconds! Before school? After school? On weekends?

Before school, I always tidy my room but I never play video games...

Practise!

A Les sons /ɪ/ ou /i:/

En anglais, il existe des sons très proches :
le son /i/ peut être **bref** comme dans *« in »* /ɪ/
ou **long** comme dans *« tea »* /i:/ (ta bouche s'étire).

1. Listen, repeat and practise! Audio 47 MP3 61

kitchen / office / tea / coffee / magazine / picture / Internet / eat / incredible / secret / need / please

2. Classify the words. Workbook p. 68

B L'accent tonique dans les mots de plusieurs syllabes

Tu as déjà vu dans l'unité 1 (p. 28) que les mots possèdent un accent tonique.

Listen, repeat and practise! Audio 48 MP3 62

1re syllabe	2e syllabe	3e syllabe
Internet **su**perpowers **ac**cess	fan**tas**tic in**cred**ible com**pu**ter	maga**zine**

C L'intonation dans les exclamations et les liaisons de mots

Dans les exclamations, la voix monte sur l'accent tonique et redescend en fin de phrase.

Listen, repeat and practise! Audio 49 MP3 63

It's nice to **see** you!

This game is fan**tas**tic!

That's in**cred**ible!

Look at that dress, it's **beau**tiful!

It's a**ma**zing!

Places in the house MP3 64

- the **en**trance door /e/
- the **kitch**en /ɪ/
- the **stu**dy /ʌ/
- the stairs /steəz/
- the **liv**ing room /ɪ/ /uː/
- the **din**ing room /aɪ/ /uː/
- the **bath**room /ˈbaːθruːm/
- a **bed**room /e/
- the **gar**den /aː/

Prepositions MP3 65

- in /ɪ/
- on /ɒ/
- **un**der /ʌ/
- in front of /ʌ/
- be**hind** /haɪ/
- be**tween** /iː/
- next to /e/ /uː/

Frequency adverbs MP3 66

- **nev**er /e/
- **some**times /ʌ/ /aɪ/
- **of**ten /ɒ/
- **al**ways /ɔː/ /eɪ/

Objects in the house MP3 67

- a com**pu**ter /juː/
- a **so**fa /əʊ/
- a **ta**ble /eɪ/
- a chair /tʃeə/
- a fridge /ɪ/
- a TV set /e/
- **flo**wers /aʊə/
- a vase /ɑː/
- a **tea**pot /iː/ /ɒ/
- a **cof**fee table /ɒ/ /eɪ/
- a lamp /æ/
- an **arm**chair /eə/
- maga**zines** /æ/ /iː/
- a **pic**ture /tʃə/

Daily routine MP3 68

- get up **ear**ly /e/ /ɜː/
- get up late /e/ /eɪ/
- go to bed /əʊ/
- stay home /eɪ/ /əʊ/
- have a snack /æ/ /æ/
- do my **home**work /əʊ/
- **ti**dy my room /aɪ/

Homework Workbook p. 70-73
Des exercices supplémentaires pour t'entraîner.

→ *Pour présenter quelqu'un, parler de ses habitudes et de ses goûts*

Le présent simple

Pour présenter quelqu'un

Amelia and Oliver live in a big house.

Pour parler de ses habitudes

Does Oliver tidy his room?
No, he doesn't.

Pour parler de ses goûts

Do you like music, Mrs Jones?
Yes, I do.

Attention à la terminaison en -s à la 3e personne du singulier.

▸ Forme affirmative

I / you / we / they + **verb**
he / she / it + **verb-s**

*He **does** the shopping.*
*She **takes** Morph out.*

▸ Forme négative

I / you / we / they + **don't**
he / she / it + **doesn't**

*He **doesn't like** shopping.*

▸ Forme interrogative et réponses courtes

Do + I / you / we / they + ...?

***Do** you **like** music?*
*Yes, I **do**.*
*No, I **don't**.*

Does + he / she + **BV**?

***Does** she **live** in Liverpool?*
*Yes, she **does**.*
*No, she **doesn't**.*

1 Scrambled sentences: put the words back into the right order.

a. the Joneses / you / know / Do / ?
b. powers / They / have / super
c. doesn't / cooking / like / Mrs Jones
d. pet/ Morph / ordinary / an / isn't

2 Answer the following questions about your family life.

a. Does your brother tidy his room every day?
b. Do you watch TV in the morning before school?
c. Do your parents play games online?
d. Do you do your homework in your bedroom?

3 Complete the paragraph about Mike.

Mike *(get up)* at 7:30 and he *(go)* to school on his bike.
He *(not / have)* school lunch so he *(take)* a lunch box.
He *(not / go)* home for lunch.
He *(play)* an instrument in the school band.

4 Write the same paragraph about you.

→ *Pour préciser la fréquence d'une action ou d'un état*

Les adverbes de fréquence

- L'adverbe de fréquence se place **devant le verbe.**
  *Mr Jones **often** hoovers.*
  *Mrs Jones **always** does the gardening.*
  *Mr and Mrs Jones **never** take Morph out.*
  *Do the twins **sometimes** tidy their room?*

- Avec **le verbe *be***, l'adverbe de fréquence se place **après**.
  *Oliver is **often** funny.*

5 Add the adverbs to the following sentences.

a. English children play instruments. *(often)*
b. They eat lunch at school. *(always)*
c. I read English magazines. *(sometimes)*
d. My cat is strange: he eats mice. *(never)*
e. My parents are strict *(often)* and they are cool. *(sometimes)*

6 Build a quiz to find out about your friend's habits. Use the following expressions:
get up early – tidy your room – ride a bike – cook

7 Write a note to your parents to prove how good you are.

a. (...) take the dog out
b. (...) do the shopping
c. (...) go to bed late
d. (...) read, (...) play video games

→ *Pour dire ce qui est présent ou non dans un endroit*

There is / there are

There is + nom au singulier
There are + nom au pluriel

Si tu énumères plusieurs choses, ton choix entre *is* et *are* ne dépendra que du premier nom de la liste.

There is a table and two armchairs in their living room.

8 What is there in Tina's bedroom?

Final Task

Domaine 2 Socle

Is your penfriend a good match? Compare your habits!

Ton projet

Ton / Ta professeur(e) organise un échange avec une école britannique. Pour que les binômes de correspondants fonctionnent bien, tu dois décrire ta maison et indiquer quelques-unes de tes habitudes. Puis, avec ton partenaire, vous imaginerez l'échange téléphonique que chacun aura avec son/sa correspondant(e).

Les étapes à suivre

STEP 1 – Individuellement

Description of your own house

- À quoi ressemble ta maison : petite, moderne… ?
- Décris quelques pièces dont ta chambre.

STEP 2 – Individuellement

Write about your habits in your house

- Fais une liste de 5 de tes habitudes.
- Indique la fréquence à l'aide d'un adverbe.

STEP 3 – En binômes

Prepare the phone conversation with your penfriend

- Réfléchis à 5 questions que tu peux poser à ton/ta correspondant(e) sur ses habitudes.
- Entraînez-vous à répondre aux questions avec ton binôme.

Bonus point! Lucky or unlucky?

- Indique si tu penses avoir un(e) correspondant(e) avec qui tu t'entendras bien ou non.
- Trouve quelques éléments pour justifier.

I BET YOU CAN!

MAINTENANT, TU ES CAPABLE DE :

- Comprendre la description d'un lieu (maison ou pièce de la maison). A1
- Comprendre la routine de quelqu'un. A1
- Présenter et décrire une maison. A1
- Parler de tes routines ou de celles d'une autre personne. A1
- Échanger des informations sur une maison. A1
- Rédiger et renseigner un questionnaire sur les habitudes. A1

Ton/ta professeur(e) te distribuera des fiches pour t'évaluer.

N'oublie pas d'utiliser :

- le lexique de la maison (p. 83)
- le lexique de la vie quotidienne (p. 83)
- le présent simple pour exprimer une habitude (p. 84)
- les adverbes de fréquence (p. 85)
- la forme interrogative du présent simple (p. 84)

Tu veux t'améliorer ?

Rends-toi page 168 à la **Banque d'exercices** et entraîne-toi à utiliser :

- *There is... / there are...*
- Le présent simple
- Les adverbes de fréquence
- Le lexique de l'unité

UNIT 5

Come to my pa

DANS CETTE UNITÉ

Tu vas découvrir

- La monnaie britannique et la nourriture
- Les fêtes d'anniversaire
- Une partie de bowling avec les jumeaux Jones

Tu seras capable de

- Dialoguer pour obtenir un prix, une date
- Écrire une date
- Faire une annonce brève
- Suivre des instructions
- Faire des suggestions à quelqu'un
- Réagir à une proposition
- Rédiger une invitation pour un anniversaire

Et tu vas

First Task ▸ Inviter un(e) ami(e) à un anniversaire

Final Task ▸ Aider Morph à s'échapper de l'appartement de Nosy Parker

ESCAPE GAME

Rhyme Time

Audio 50

MP3 69

Happy birthday

Happy birthday to you,
Happy birthday to you.
Today is a great day,
Because it's your birthday.
Now it's time to celebrate,
With a giant birthday cake.
Now, blow out the candles,
1, 2, 3, very simple.
Happy birthday to you,
I wish you all the best,
Have fun with all your guests! (x2)

Pupils' Interactive Activities

My Karaoke!
Entraîne-toi à chanter avec ton karaoké !

rty!

"Alice in Wonderland", a Tim Burton film

Re-cycle!

Remember?

Compétences
- Comprendre une liste de courses.
- Dialoguer pour obtenir un prix.

1. What do you need for your birthday party?

a. Listen to the food items on the shopping list. Repeat and memorise them. Audio 51

ba**na**nas /bəˈnɑːnəz/

strawberries /ˈstrɔːbərɪz/

apples /ˈæpəlz/

pears /peərz/

to**ma**toes /təˈmɑːtəʊz/

peas /piːz/

crisps /ɪ/

po**ta**toes /pəˈteɪtəʊz/

carrots /ˈkærəts/

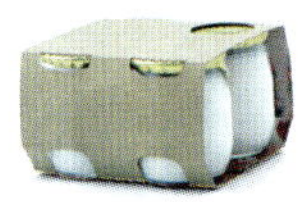
yoghurt /ˈjɒgət/

eggs /egz/

cheese /tʃiːz/

mushrooms /ˈmʌʃruːmz/

ham /hæm/

pancakes /æ/ /eɪ/

milk /mɪlk/

ice cream /aɪ/ /iː/

fizzy drink /ɪ/ /i/

b. Tick the pictures corresponding to your shopping lists in your workbook. Workbook p. 74

2. Do you like sweet treats?

a. Look, listen and repeat the prices. Audio 52

b. What can you buy with £2?
Example: *I can buy mints and 4 chocolate bars and...*

c. Play a game of bingo with British coins and notes. Workbook p. 75

Help!

£1 (pound) = 100p (pence) /piː/ /e/

3. Have it your way for your birthday!

Order pizzas and smoothies and choose extra ingredients.
Listen to the example and play with your partner. Audio 53

"I would like a regular pizza, please."
"Would you like extra ingredients?"
"Yes, please. I would like ham and onion."
"Here you are. That's £9."

Help!
A polite way to ask for a pizza:
I would like a pizza, please.

Regular Pizza £8	Regular Smoothie £4

Extra ingredients 50p ham / mushroom / cheese / peas / onion / bacon / olives	Extra ingredients 50p strawberries / pear / apple / banana

4. At the sweet shop

Workbook p. 76

a. Listen to the dialogue and do the activity in your workbook. Audio 54 MP3 70

b. Now, do your shopping at the sweet shop. Interact with your friend.

Customer: *Hello!*
Cashier: *Hi!*
Customer: *I'd like some sweets for my birthday party, how much are the mints?*
Cashier: *They are 40p.*
Customer: *Okay, thank you! And how much is a donut?*
Cashier: *It is 80p.*
Customer: *Great, thanks! Can I have a bag of mints and 5 donuts please?*
Cashier: *No problem, that is £4.40.*
Customer: *Here you are! Bye!*
Cashier: *Thank you! See you!*

A traditional sweet shop in York

Help!
- Pour connaître le prix d'un article : *How much **is it**?*
- Pour connaître le prix de plusieurs articles : *How much **are they**?*

Lesson 1 DISCOVER
My birthday party

Compétences
- Dialoguer pour obtenir une date.
- Inviter des amis à une fête.
- Comprendre un projet.

1. Happy birthday!

Help!

03/12

= *December 3rd*
= *March 12th*

Help!

1st = the fir**st**
21st = the twenty-fir**st**
2nd = the **second**
22nd = the twenty-**second**
/k/
3rd = the **third**
23rd = the twenty-**third**
4th = the four**th**
24th = the twenty-four**th**
5th = the **fifth**
25th = the twenty-fif**th**
/ɪ/

a. Listen and point at the corresponding personalities. Audio 55

b. Now listen to other famous people and write down their birthdays. Audio 56 Workbook p. 77

c. Work in groups and complete the birthday calendar. Workbook p. 78

d. Play the "Birthday Memory Game". Workbook p. 78

e. Write the dates in English and American. Workbook p. 79

2. Nick's birthday party

Video 08

a. Watch Nick's video. Identify the different steps to organise a party.

b. Match each step with its label. Workbook p. 79

c. Recap what Nick needs.
Example: *He needs some… but he doesn't need any…*

Help!

- Pour désigner une grande quantité
  a lot of + nom
- Pour désigner un **indénombrable** ou une **quantité indéfinie** :
  some + nom
- Si la phrase est **négative** :
  any + nom

3. Invite your friend

a. Listen to the three messages on the voice mailbox and take notes. **Audio 57-59** **Workbook p. 80**

b. Look at the invitation card. What's missing?
Go to your workbook and complete the card. **Workbook p. 80**

Dear Jane,
I'm organising my birthday party next week,
on February 10th. I hope you're free and you can come…
I'm planning a Star Wars party so I'm cooking
a Master Yoda cake. I'm buying some coke
and Chewbacca balloons. I'm inviting Kevin.
He's buying some fruit juice.
Can you bring sweets?
See ya!
xxx
Olivia

Help!
birthday
on February 10th

4. Send an invitation

First Task

You're organising your birthday party.
Write an invitation to your friend or leave a message.
Choose one of the cards below and prepare your message.
(Use the model in activity 3.)

★ **JACK'S BIRTHDAY**

WHEN: next month-Saturday 15th
PARTY THEME: video games
FOOD: brownies and lemonade

★★ **LEILA'S BIRTHDAY**

WHEN: next Friday afternoon – May 17th
PARTY THEME: hip hop
FOOD: muffins and fruit juice
MUSIC: ?

★★★ **JESSICA'S BIRTHDAY**

WHEN: ?
PARTY THEME:

FOOD:

Lesson 1 | GO FURTHER
Festive food

Compétences
- Suivre des instructions.
- Exprimer ses goûts.
- Comprendre une bande dessinée.

1. A recipe: how to make scones

Read the recipe and reorder the pictures.

You need:

14 tablespoons flour
3 tablespoons sugar
1 teaspoon baking powder
½ teaspoon salt
60 g butter
60 g raisins
½ glass of milk

6 STEPS

1. Mix together the flour, the salt, the sugar and the baking powder. Then add the raisins and the butter.
2. Add the milk to form the dough into a ball.
3. Roll the dough out into a 2.5 cm thick round.
4. Cut the dough into circles.
5. Bake in a hot oven for 15 minutes.
6. Enjoy your scones!

2. Bertie Botts's every flavour beans

a. These jellybeans are special. Do you know why? Do you know who Bertie Bott is?

b. Look at the flavours: What is your favourite flavour? Is it yummy or yucky?

3. Happy birthday Garfield!

a. What is special today at Garfield's?

b. Look at the different pictures: is Garfield happy? surprised? angry? tired?

Garfield, Sunday, June 19th, 1994 © Paws Inc.

Lesson 2 Story TIME

Compétences
- Donner des instructions (obligations et interdictions).
- Faire des propositions à quelqu'un.

Bowling is fun!

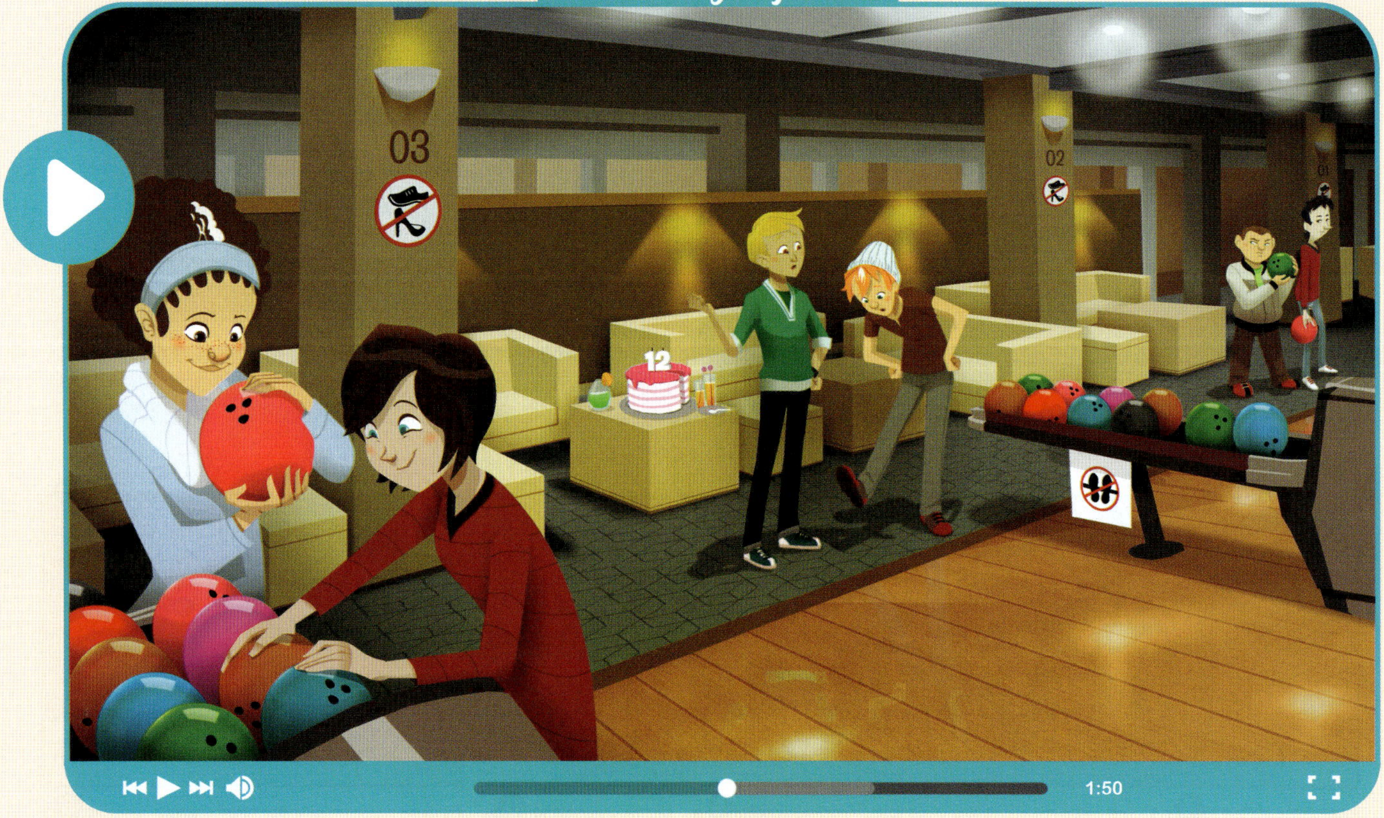

1. Get ready

a. Look at the picture and say what you can.

2. Watch the episode Video 09

a. Watch the video **(sound off).** Match the characters with one or more feelings.
Workbook p. 81
Example: *I think Sophia is excited because she loves bowling.*

b. Listen to the first part of the document **(video off)**. Pick out one word to justify your choice.

c. Concentrate on the repetitions. What words are repeated?
Workbook p. 81

d. Read the poster in your workbook and answer the questions. Workbook p. 82

3. Act out! MP3 71

a. Practise acting. Workbook p. 83

b. Memorise and act out the scene.

Help!

must + BV
= obligation
mustn't + BV
= interdiction

Pupils' Interactive Activities

Act out!
- Prépare ton rôle avec le karaoké.
- Ton/ta professeur(e) te donnera le code pour revoir l'épisode.

4. Is Kari a good babysitter? Audio 60

a. Listen and match the expressions with the corresponding pictures.

phone and reas**sure** the **pa**rents | **pan**ic | play with the kid

play with fire / play **dan**gerous games | play loud **mu**sic | make a mess

1

2

3

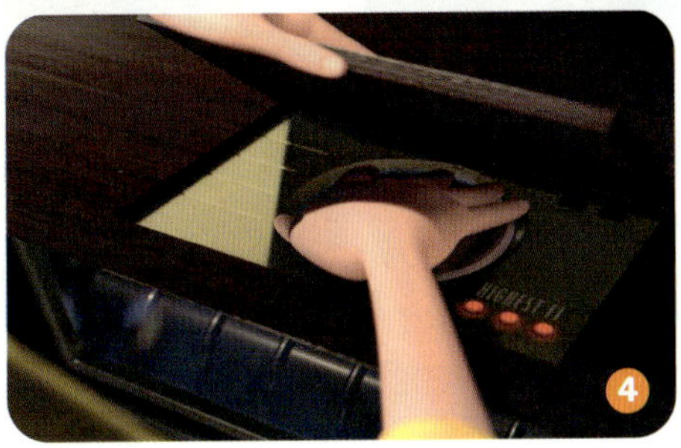
4

5

b. In your opinion, is Kari a good babysitter?

A good babysitter must...

A good babysitter mustn't...

Help!

Mustn't + BV

c. Go to your workbook and complete the note Bob and Helen Parr wrote to Kari. Workbook p. 84

5. The "adorable" cousins

Mr and Mrs Jones are at the cinema with uncle Mike and his wife. Oliver offers to babysit his terrible little cousins in the evening.

a. Go to your workbook and imagine the conversation.
Workbook p. 85

b. Listen to the cousins and imagine Oliver's answers.
Audio 61

6. Play roles

Choose a character (Oliver or the terrible cousins) and imagine the conversation (3 suggestions and reactions).

Help!

Demander la permission :
Can + sujet + BV?

HAVE FUN IN GROUPS

Play the "What are the Cambridges doing?" game

1. Speaking Décrire une activité et échanger des renseignements

How to play ⌛ 5/10 min

★

Pupil A says *"William is playing polo."*
Pupil B points at the corresponding picture and says: *"Yes, look! William is playing polo in picture 1."*

★★

Pupil A points at a picture and says: *"What is Kate doing in picture 3?"*
Pupil B: *"Kate is laughing."*

Help Yourself!

2. Reading — Comprendre un texte illustré

→ En s'appuyant sur les images et sur les signes de ponctuation.
→ En repérant les mots connus.
→ En identifiant les personnages.

Choose your activity and go to your workbook.

★ Workbook p. 86

★★ Workbook p. 86

★★★ Workbook p. 86

A MAD TEA PARTY

PART 1 People and place

There is a very big table under a tree in front of the house. The March Hare and the Hatter are at the table, having tea. There is a Dormouse between them, he is asleep. Alice sits in a large chair at one end of the very long table.

PART 2 Drinks

"Have some wine" says the March Hare to Alice.
"But there's only tea, I don't see any wine!" says Alice.
"It's not very polite to sit down when you are not invited" the March Hare answers.

PART 3 Conversation

"Is it your table?" Alice asks.
"It's a very long table just for three people."
Then the Hatter says "Your hair is too long."
Alice is angry. "Don't make personal remarks! It's very impolite!"
Then the Hatter asks "What day of the month is it?"
"The fourth." Alice says.
The Hatter is angry.
"My watch is two days wrong!".
He puts his watch into his cup of tea.
"This is a very stupid tea party!
I'm going now." Alice says.

Adapted from Alice's Adventures in Wonderland
by ***Lewis Carroll*** *(1865).*
Illustrated by Sir John Tenniel.

Language Lab *Words & Sounds*

Pupils' Interactive Activities

Entraîne-toi avec les exercices interactifs.

Memorise the words!

1 Food
Ask and answer questions about your favourite food.

2 Miming a feeling
Guess the feeling/emotion your partner is miming.

3 Action time
Listen to your friend and complete the action.

Practise!

A Les sons longs
Après avoir étudié /iː/ comme dans « *peas* », où la longueur du son est symbolisée par deux points, tu vas découvrir d'autres sons longs de l'anglais.

1. Listen, repeat and practise! Audio 62 MP3 72

/iː/	p**ea**s – ch**ee**se	/uː/	j**u**ice – f**oo**d – sm**oo**thie
/ɔː/	str**aw**berries – **o**rganise	/ɑː/	ban**a**nas – p**a**rty

2. Read the words aloud. What's the odd one? Audio 63 MP3 73

a. *carrots – cat – card*
b. *four – dog – yoghurt*
c. *book – choose – look*
d. *crisps – pizza – tea*

B Les mots accentués sur la dernière syllabe
Listen, repeat and practise! Audio 64 MP3 74

*sur**prised** – an**noyed** – pre**pare** – se**lect** – in**vite***

C Les interjections en anglais
S'il existe des interjections dans toutes les langues, elles ne se prononcent pas toutes de la même manière !

Listen, repeat and practise! Audio 65 MP3 75

***Ooh,** I love bowling!*
***Aww!** I prefer my trainers!*
***Er,** Millie?*
***Ugh!** I hate those guys!*
***Oy!** Blake is eating our birthday cake!*
***Ouch!** I cut my finger!*

D La prononciation du son « th »
Il existe deux prononciations.

/θ/	/ð/
bathroom	mother

Listen to the words and classify them into the right column. Audio 66 MP3 76 Workbook p. 88

three – Thursday – thirteen – thirty – fourth – twenty-seventh – theme – think – weather – they – that – this – father

Food MP3 77

- ba**na**nas /ɑː/
- **straw**berries /ɔː/
- pears /eə/
- to**ma**toes /ɑː/
- peas /iː/
- po**ta**toes /eɪ/
- **mush**rooms /ʌ/ /uː/
- **yog**hurt /jɒ/
- cheese /iː/
- ham /æ/
- **ba**con /eɪ/
- **piz**za /iː/
- a **birth**day cake /ɜː/ /eɪ/
- snacks /æ/
- **pan**cakes /æ/ /eɪ/
- a **smoo**thie /uː/
- juice /ʤuːs/
- crisps /ɪ/

Money MP3 78

- a pound (£) /aʊ/
- a **pen**ny (p.) /e/

coins /kɔɪnz/

- a bank note /əʊ/

Emotions MP3 79

- ex**ci**ted /ɪk'saɪtɪd/
- an**noyed** /ɔɪd/
- sur**prised** /aɪ/
- **mock**ing /ɒ/
- **an**gry /æ/

Actions MP3 80

pre**pare** / **or**ganise a **par**ty /eə/ /ɔː/ /aɪ/ /ɑː/

in**vite** friends /aɪ/

write cards /aɪ/ /ɑː/

choose deco**ra**tions /ʧuːz/ /eɪ/

se**lect mu**sic /e/ /juː/

buy food /aɪ/ /uː/

celebrate my **birth**day /e/ /eɪ/ /eɪ/

bring snacks /æ/

reas**sure pa**rents /ʃɔː/ /eə/

play loud **mu**sic /aʊ/

make a mess /eɪ/ /e/

light **can**dles /æ/

Homework Workbook p. 90-93
Des exercices supplémentaires pour t'entraîner.

→ Pour exprimer une obligation ou une interdiction

Must + BV

Ce qui est obligatoire.

*You **must** change your shoes.*

Mustn't + BV

Ce qui est interdit.

*You **mustn't** cross the black line.*

1 The teacher is angry today because his/her pupils are not very serious.
Complete what he/she says with must or mustn't.

Now stop it, please. You ... sit down but you ... swing on your chair! Alex, you ... eat chewing gum. No Alex, you ... stick it under the table, please! Now children, you ... concentrate!

2 Say what you must or mustn't do at the museum.

a.

b.

c.

d.

→ Pour s'informer sur une date ou un prix

Sur une date

On utilise le mot interrogatif **when**.

***When** is your birthday? It's **in** May. It's **on** the 24th.*

***When** are you organising a party? On Saturday.*

Sur un prix

On utilise le mot interrogatif **how much**.

***How much** are the cupcakes?*

***How much** is the pizza?*

3 Find Amelia's questions to Ollie to get the dates for:

- Grandmas birthday
- Maths test
- Cousins coming
- Cinema with Ollie

4 You've got £4 in your purse. Ask questions to check what you can buy for your party.

(= 80p)

→ Pour exprimer une action en train de se dérouler ou que l'on a prévue

Be + V-ing

On utilise ***be*** au présent suivi du verbe terminé en ***-ing***.

- Si le verbe se termine par un ***e***, celui-ci disparaît. *come* → *com**ing***
- Si le verbe a une seule syllabe ou se termine par une syllabe accentuée, on double la consonne finale.

  run → ***run**ning*
  begin → *begi**nn**ing*

Attention : *listen* → *listening*

*Are you busy? Yes, I **am** organis**ing** a party.*

*My friends **are** com**ing** to my party on Saturday.*

Avec un verbe au présent ***be* + V-*ing*** :

- on peut décrire une activité en cours, une situation présente.
  *Where's Nick? In his room. He'**s** phon**ing** a friend.*
- on peut exprimer un projet planifié.
  *Nick **is** hav**ing** a party tomorrow for his birthday.*

Forme affirmative

Sujet + am/is/are + V-ing

Forme négative

Sujet + am not/isn't/aren't + V-ing

Forme interrogative

am/is/are + sujet + V-ing

5 **Look at the picture and describe what is happening.**

6 **Write the verbs in the present *Be* + V-*ing*.**

a. – Can you see Simon and Blake?
– Yes, they (play) ... on lane two.
– Ah, OK! But look, Simon (cross) ... the black line. He (not / pay) ... attention.
– I think they (respect / not) ... the rules.

b. – Hi Zoey! Is your brother in?
– No, he (play) ... outside with his mates.
– What (they / do) ... ?
– They (train) ... because they (run) ... the city marathon next week.
– Oh, I see! So they (come / not) ... to my party!

7 **Amelia is busy this week. What is she doing?**

Monday	Tuesday	Wednesday	Thursday	Friday	Saturday	Sunday

Final Task

Domaine 2 Socle

Help Morph escape Nosy Parker!

ESCAPE GAME

TEACHER'S SLIDES

Votre projet

Nosy Parker a réussi à capturer Morph ! Il le détient dans une cage. Pour pouvoir emmener Morph avec vous à la fête d'anniversaire, aidez-le à s'enfuir.

Les étapes à suivre

STEP 1

Morph is locked in a cage

Aidez Morph à se transformer en souris pour qu'il passe entre les barreaux de sa cage.

STEP 2

Morph is now free from the cage

Mais où a lieu la fête d'anniversaire ? Déchiffrez le code et remplissez le carton d'invitation.

STEP 3

Morph is still locked inside the flat

Aidez-le à se transformer en coccinelle pour qu'il puisse se glisser sous la porte de l'appartement.

I BET YOU CAN!

MAINTENANT, TU ES CAPABLE DE :

- Comprendre des mots familiers et expressions courantes sur la nourriture. A1
- Suivre des instructions. A1
- Décrire une activité. A1
- Faire une brève annonce. A1
- Demander une permission. A1
- Échanger des informations sur un prix, une date. A1
- Suivre des instructions (obligations et interdictions). A1
- Écrire une date. A1
- Rédiger une invitation. A1
- Comprendre un texte court et illustré. A2
- Réagir à des propositions et faire des suggestions. A2

Ton/ta professeur(e) te distribuera des fiches pour t'évaluer.

N'oublie pas d'utiliser :

- le lexique des actions (p. 97)
- le lexique de la nourriture (p. 90, 101)
- des verbes d'action (p. 97)
- *must* et *mustn't* (p. 102)
- le présent *be* + V-*ing* (p. 103)

Tu veux t'améliorer ?

Rends-toi p. 170 à la **Banque d'exercices** et entraîne-toi à utiliser :

- Les quantités
- *Must / Mustn't*
- Le present *Be + V-ing*
- Les prépositions
- Le lexique de l'unité

UNIT 6

From London

DANS CETTE UNITÉ

Tu vas découvrir

- Des lieux emblématiques de Londres
- Quelques repères géographiques aux États-Unis
- L'inoubliable sortie scolaire des jumeaux Jones

Tu seras capable de

- Lire et comprendre des informations sur les monuments de Londres
- Comprendre un itinéraire
- Chercher des informations sur un site internet
- Exprimer un choix
- Décrire les lieux d'une ville
- Raconter un événement, une histoire courte
- Rédiger une carte postale

Et tu vas

First Task ▸ Déterminer le programme des visites pour un voyage à Londres

Final Task ▸ Réaliser un carnet de voyage

Rhyme Time

Audio 67

MP3 81

Let's go to London!
Come on, let's go to London!
There's no sun but a lot of fun.
Look! It's nine past ten,
On that old Big Ben.
Never, never mind the rain,
Just take the train, the train!
And don't make a fuss,
Hop on a bus! a bus!
Come on, let's go to London! (x2)

Pupils' Interactive Activities

My Karaoke!
Entraîne-toi à chanter avec ton karaoké !

to the States

The London skyline: past and present

Re-cycle!

Remember?

Compétences
- Identifier des modes de transport.
- Repérer des lieux et les décrire simplement.
- Comprendre un itinéraire.

1. Transport in London

Write the names of the different means of transport in London. Workbook p. 94

a.

b.

c.

d.

e.

f.

2. London landmarks

Look at the map. Identify and count the different types of landmarks.

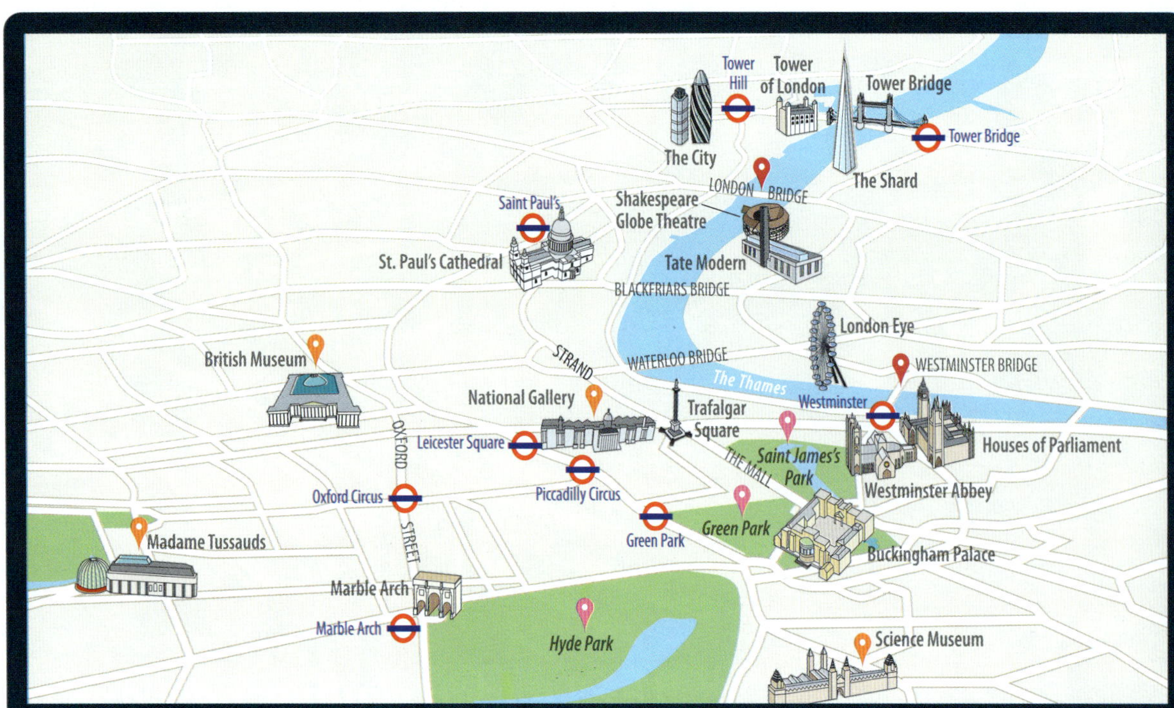

3. A sightseeing tour

Audio 68 Workbook p. 95-96

a. Listen to the guide. Identify the places you can see on the bus tour. Number them in the correct order.

b. Listen again, take notes and write a sentence to describe two places of your choice.
Example: *This is Westminster: there is Big Ben and the Houses of Parliament. The building is long.*

Help!
- On the left ↰
- On the right ↱

4. Guessing game

Pairwork: Guess the landmark your partner is thinking of.

Lesson 1 DISCOVER
London landmarks

Compétences
- Comprendre un texte informatif.
- Trouver des informations sur internet.
- Exprimer ce que l'on souhaite faire.

1. The river bus ride

Read the leaflet. Then go to your workbook and do the activities. Workbook p. 97-98

Do you like acting?

The Globe Theatre is a very famous theatre in London. It's round and it has no roof. You can enjoy a play by William Shakespeare.

The Globe

The London Eye

Do you like adventure?

The London Eye is a giant wheel on the River Thames in London. The structure is 443 feet (135 m) tall and the wheel has a diameter of 394 feet (120 m). The wheel has 32 passenger capsules and gives an extraordinary view over the city.

Do you like science?

The Royal Observatory is in Greenwich Park, near the River Thames. You can discover the world of astronomy and navigation, and also stand on the Prime Meridian.

Greenwhich Observatory

Do you like shopping?

Take the tube to Camden Town or the boat along Regent's Canal. Camden is a big market for vintage clothes, shoes, music. You can buy souvenirs there!

Camden Lock

THE RIVER BUS RIDE

The Olympic Village

Do you like sports?

Queen Elizabeth Olympic Park is the 2012 Summer Olympic sports complex. In the park, there is the Olympic Village, the London Stadium and the London Aquatics Centre.

2. Things to do

a. Go on the internet and copy the website address given by your teacher. Find information about these museums (opening times, etc.). Workbook p. 98

b. Use the information to present one of the places.
The science museum is free and it's open from... to... You can see...

VISITLONDON.COM

The Science Museum

Madame Tussauds

The Natural History Museum

The Harry Potter Studios

3. What would you like to do? Audio 69

Listen to the dialogue and recap what the pupils would like to do in London.
Example: *Lisa would like to... because she likes...*
Tom would like to... because he...

Help!

Pour exprimer ce que tu souhaites faire :
I would like to + base verbale.
Attention, dans « would » /wʊd/,
la lettre « l » ne se prononce pas.

4. A weekend in London

First Task

Have a look at all the possible activities for your school trip to London. Choose one and explain your choice to your group. Decide on the best one and report to the class.

Lesson 1 GO FURTHER
London or New York?

Compétences
- Repérer des éléments culturels.
- Exprimer un choix.

1. Covent Garden, the place to be!

a. What does the picture tell you about Covent Garden?

b. What street performer would you like to see? Why?
A juggler? A contortionist? A fire-eater? A tightrope-walker? An acrobat? A unicyclist? A magician?

2. Times Square is awesome!

a. Identify four elements indicating that it's in New York City.

b. Where would you like to go to? London or New York?

Lesson 2 Story TIME

Compétences
- Comprendre un événement passé.
- Raconter son week-end.

The informers

1. Get ready

Look at the title of the episode and at the picture and say what you can.

Help!
BE au prétérit
I / he / she / it **was**
we / you / they **were**

2. Watch the episode

Video 10

a. Watch the first part and check your ideas.

b. Watch again. Do the activities in your workbook. Workbook p. 99

c. Recap what happened.

d. How does Nosy Parker react to the phone conversation?

3. Act out!

MP3 82 Workbook p. 100

a. Practise acting.

b. Memorise and act out the scene.

Pupils' Interactive Activities

Act out!
- Prépare ton rôle avec le karaoké.
- Ton/ta professeur(e) te donnera le code pour revoir l'épisode.

4. An amazing weekend!

Tim and Sophia had an amazing weekend with the twins. Oliver teleported them across the USA.

a. Look at the map. Talk about their activities.

b. Listen to the conversation and complete the programme in your workbook. Audio 70 Workbook p. 101

c. Use your notes to write about their weekend.

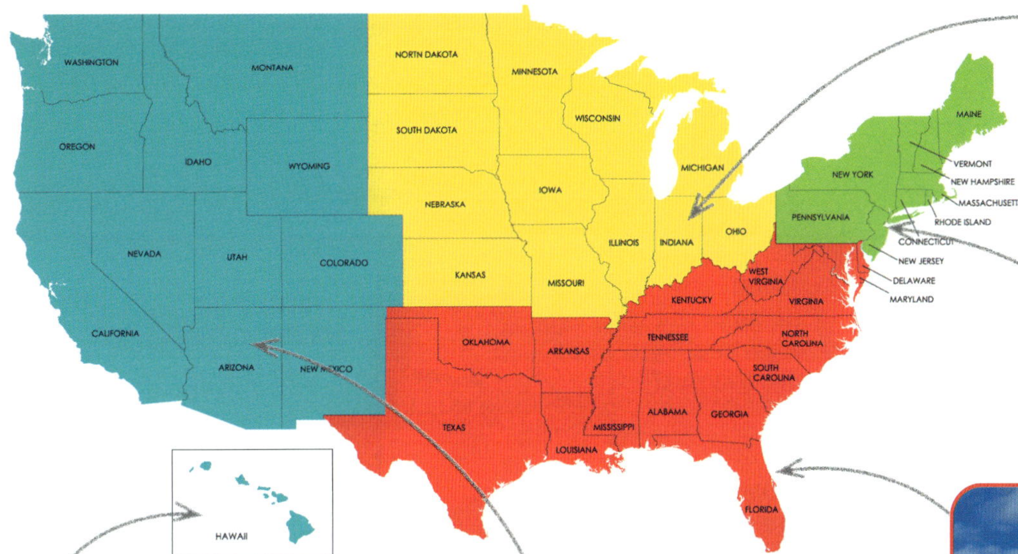

5. A terrible weekend!

a. Pairwork: Morph and Oliver feel terrible this Monday morning. Guess what they did last weekend. Example: *Did Oliver ... ?*
Use the worksheets your teacher will give you.

b. Recap Morph and Ollie's weekend.

Time to think

Le prétérit

- **Verbes réguliers**
  V + -ed = visited
- **Verbes irréguliers**
  go → went
  take (photos) → took
  have (food and drink) → had

HAVE FUN IN GROUPS

Play "The tour guide" game

How to play ⌛ 30 min

* In pairs or 2 to 3 teams of different levels. Roll the dice and answer the questions. Look at the pictures, they can help you!

⭐ Answer the questions in green.

⭐⭐ Answer the questions in green and yellow.

⭐⭐⭐ Answer all the questions.

1. Speaking Donner des renseignements

You can play with all levels or choose a level.
You can also compete with someone or a team of a different level.

What colour are London taxis?	Where can you find 775 rooms?	What is the name of the big wheel by the Thames?		What colour are the phone booths?	Finish here!
I can open and close, I'm a bridge.		What colour are double-decker buses?		It was a prison, now it's a castle and a museum.	
Where did you see a dinosaur?		Give the name of the river in London.		What colour are the squirrels in London?	
What is the other name of the Underground?		What colour is the Gherkin?		Where did you see giant lions?	
What is the Globe?		Who is Kate Middleton?		Which bell can you hear ringing every 15 minutes?	
Start here!		Where did you go shopping?	When did London host the Olympic Games?	Where does the Queen live?	

Help Yourself!

2. Interacting Dialoguer pour obtenir des renseignements et faire un choix

→ En mobilisant tes connaissances lexicales et grammaticales.
→ En coopérant et en s'entraidant dans le cadre d'un travail de groupe.

Workbook p. 102-103

- **Individually**

Find the activities.

- **Pairwork**

A bad or a good weekend? Decide and create a card with your partner.

- **Groupwork**

Ask your friends questions about their cards. Answer their questions.
Did Millie have a good or a bad weekend?

3. Writing Rédiger une carte postale

→ En mobilisant tes connaissances lexicales et grammaticales.
→ En respectant le format d'une carte postale (présentation et formules de politesse).

Go to your workbook to write your postcard. Workbook p. 104-105

★ Write two things that you did and two things that you didn't do.

★★ Write four things that you did and two things that you didn't do.

★★★ Write five things that you did and three things that you didn't do.

Language Lab Words & Sounds

Pupils' Interactive Activities

Entraîne-toi avec les exercices interactifs.

Memorise the words!

1 Transport and places

Describe your city/village.

2 Look at the map!

Use the maps in your textbook to locate places in Great Britain and in the USA.

London is in the South...

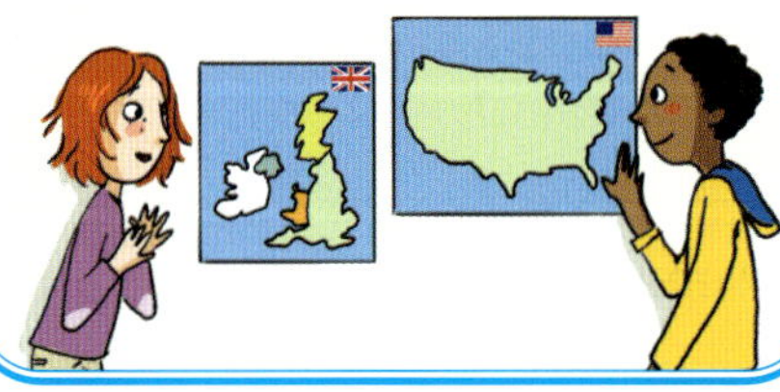

3 Where is it?

Pupil A: "Where is Tower Bridge?"

Pupil B: "It's in London / England"

Practise!

A La prononciation des verbes au prétérit

1. Listen, repeat and practise. Audio 71 MP3 83

- We played beach volleyball.
  /d/
- We relaxed in Hawaii and we surfed.
  /t/ /t/
- We visited the Statue of Liberty.
  /ɪd/

2. Listen and classify the verbs. Audio 72 MP3 84

Workbook p. 106

3. Find the verb base of those verbs. Pronounce the pairs.

Example: *teleported* → *teleport*

visited – relaxed – surfed – played – watched – decided – liked – opened – listened

B La prononciation des lieux célèbres

Il te faut bien connaître leur prononciation !

Listen, repeat and practise! Audio 73 MP3 85

London /ʌ/	**Buck**ingham **Pal**ace /ʌ/ /æ/	Tra**fal**gar **Square** /æ/ /skweə/
New **York** /njuːˈjɔːrk/	St Paul's Ca**the**dral /θiː/	Chi**ca**go /ʃɪˈkɑːgəʊ/
Ha**wai**i /həˈwaɪiː/	**Stat**ue of **Lib**erty /juː/ /ə/	Grand **Can**yon /ˈkænjən/

C La prononciation de la lettre « a ».

Listen, repeat and practise! Audio 74 MP3 86

- letter a = sound /æ/
  Palace – Trafalgar – Statue – Grand Canyon
- letter a = sound /ə/
  Palace – cathedral – Hawaii – Buckingham
- letter a = sound /ɑː/
  Parliament – Chicago

Transport MP3 87

a **bi**cycle
/aɪ/

a train
/eɪ/

a **riv**er bus
/ɪ/ /ʌ/

a **tax**i
/æ/

the **un**derground
/ʌ/ /aʊ/

a tube **sta**tion
/uː/ /'steɪʃən/

a **dou**ble-**deck**er bus
/ʌ/ /ʌ/

Inside museums MP3 90

modern art
/ɒ/ /ɑː/

jewels
/'ʤuːəlz/

ce**leb**rities
/e/

as**tron**omy
/ɒ/

a **di**nosaur
/'daɪnəsɔː/

Places MP3 88

a mu**se**um
/mjuː'zɪəm/

a **riv**er
/ɪ/
a bridge
/ɪ/

a park
/pɑːk/

a wheel
/iː/

a **thea**tre
/θɪə/

a **tow**er
/'taʊər/

buildings
/ɪ/

a **sta**dium
/eɪ/

a **vil**lage
/'vɪlɪʤ/

a roof
/uː/

Locating a place MP3 89

North
/ɔː/

West
/e/

East
/iː/

South
/aʊ/

on the right
/aɪ/

on the left
/e/

A visitor's kit MP3 91

a **back**pack
/æ/ /æ/

a **tick**et
/ɪ/ /ɪ/

a **leaf**let
/iː/

a map
/æ/

Activities MP3 92

dis**cov**er **Lon**don
/ɪ/ /'lʌndən/

visit a mu**se**um
/ɪ/ /mjuːzɪəm/

take **pho**tos
/eɪ/ /əʊ/

do some **shop**ping
/ɒ/

buy a souve**nir**
/aɪ/ /uː/

Homework Workbook p. 108-112
Des exercices supplémentaires pour t'entraîner.

→ *Pour exprimer un souhait, un désir*

Would like to + BV

Forme affirmative pleine

*I **would like to** visit the Harry Potter Studios.*

Forme affirmative contractée

*I**'d like to** visit the Harry Potter Studios.*

La forme interrogative

Would passe devant le sujet.

*What **would you like to** do?*

***Would you like to** go to Camden Town?*

1 Ann is planning a trip to New York with her parents. Complete their conversation, using *would like to + verbal base.* Choose the right verb in the list:
visit – do – eat – watch – go

"Ann, what (you / ...) in New York?"

"I (...) a match, I love baseball!"

"What about museums? (...) the Museum of Modern Art?"

"No, thanks but I (...) to the Statue of Liberty! And I (...) in a Mexican restaurant, I love tacos!"

2 Jenny had a bad week at school. To comfort her, her parents asked her to make a list of what she'd like to do at the weekend. Look at her list and recap.

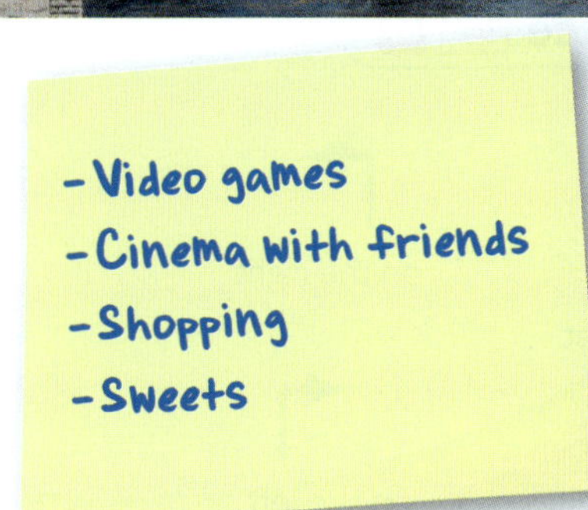

→ *Pour raconter un événement passé*

Le prétérit

Les verbes réguliers

Verb + -<u>ed</u>

*We **visit<u>ed</u>** London last week.*

Les verbes irréguliers

Ce sont les verbes qui prennent une forme particulière au prétérit. Il faut les apprendre par cœur. Tu en as vu 3 dans cette unité :

*We **had*** (have) *a fantastic weekend.*

*We **went*** (go) *to New York.*

*We **took*** (take) *photos.*

L'auxiliaire BE

La forme affirmative

I / he / she / it **was**
/wɒz/

we / you / they **were**
/wɜː/

La forme négative

I / he / she / it **wasn't**

we / you / they **weren't**
/wɜːnt/

La forme interrogative

Pour poser une question à laquelle <u>on répond par oui ou par non</u>, on utilise ***did*** (prétérit de l'auxiliaire *do*).

***Did** you visit Mme Tussauds?*
*<u>Yes</u>, I **did**. / <u>No</u>, I **didn't**.*

La forme négative

On utilise ***didn't*** (= *did not*).

*We **didn't** visit the White House.*

3 **Complete with the correct form of *be*: was / wasn't or were / weren't.**

a. Michael Jackson (...) a famous singer. He (...) British, he (...) American.

b. The Beatles (...) a famous English group. They (...) from Liverpool.

c. Princess Diana (...) Prince Charles's first wife. She (...) beautiful.

d. (...) you at school yesterday? No / I (...) at home.

4 **Complete the life story of William Shakespeare with:**
have (x2) – **live** (x2) – **be** (x2) – **like** (x1) – **go** (x1)

Shakespeare was a great writer. He (...) English. He (...) a theatre in London called the Globe. His wife (...) Ann Hathaway. They (...) three children. They were separated: Shakespeare (...) in London, but his wife (...) in Stratford-upon-Avon with their children. Queen Elizabeth 1st (...) Shakespeare's plays. She sometimes (...) to the theatre.

Final Task

Domaine 2 Socle

Present your amazing trip

Your project

Tu es de retour d'un voyage à Londres (ou une autre destination en Grande-Bretagne ou aux États-Unis). Choisis des photos et raconte de manière simple ce que tu as fait ou pas lors de ton voyage. Tu peux le faire sous la forme d'un diaporama commenté ou d'un journal de voyage papier.

Follow the steps

STEP 1

What did you visit?

Sélectionne cinq lieux que tu as visités et leur photo. Réalise un diaporama ou un collage avec ces photos. Note le lieu et/ou le nom du monument.

STEP 2

Say what you did!

Pour chaque lieu, prépare une liste des choses que tu as faites et des adjectifs pour exprimer tes réactions.

STEP 3

Practise presenting your trip!

Utilise tes notes et entraîne-toi à raconter ce que tu as fait (ou pas) dans chaque lieu.

STEP 4

Create and present your trip!

Option 1 : Enregistre ton récit sur le diaporama que tu as créé.

Option 2 : Présente ton voyage à l'oral.

I BET YOU CAN!

MAINTENANT, TU ES CAPABLE DE :

- Comprendre un itinéraire. **A1**
- Comprendre un événement passé. **A1**
- Décrire un lieu. **A1**
- Exprimer un choix parmi une liste d'activités. **A1**
- Isoler des informations simples dans un court texte. **A1**
- Raconter un événement passé. **A2**
- Échanger des informations sur un week-end passé. **A2**
- Repérer des informations ciblées sur un document informatif. **A2**
- Écrire une courte description d'activités passées dans une carte postale. **A2**

Ton/ta professeur(e) te distribuera des fiches pour t'évaluer.

N'oublie pas d'utiliser :

- le lexique des lieux et des monuments (p. 119)
- le lexique des activités (p. 119)
- le prétérit pour raconter ce que tu as fait ou visité (p. 121)

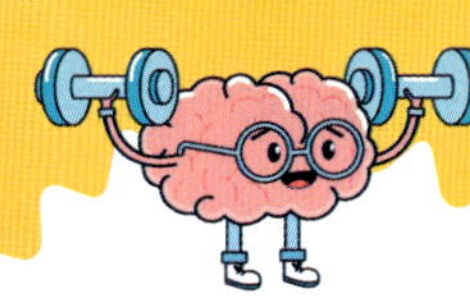

Tu veux t'améliorer ?

Rends-toi p. 172 à la **Banque d'exercices** et entraîne-toi à utiliser :

- *Would like to* + BV
- Le prétérit
- Le lexique de l'unité

UNIT 7

Let's have a br

DANS CETTE UNITÉ

Tu vas découvrir

- Les activités de loisirs, en particulier celles de plein air
- Le séjour de la famille Jones dans un parc de loisirs

Tu seras capable de

- Comprendre et énumérer des activités de loisirs
- Extraire l'information essentielle d'une conversation
- Faire des suggestions
- Réagir à des propositions et donner ton avis
- Comprendre le contenu d'un dépliant publicitaire
- Suivre la trame narrative d'une bande dessinée
- Comprendre les projets de quelqu'un

Et tu vas

Final Task ▸ Imaginer un camp de vacances et réaliser une annonce publicitaire radio

Rhyme Time

Audio 75

MP3 93

Let's have some fun!

Let's have some fun!
Why don't you run?
Kick the ball or play basketball... (x2)
Let's have some fun! (x2)
Don't you enjoy swimming?
Do you prefer horse riding?
Let's have some fun! (x2)
Grab your racket...
Or let's play cricket...
Let's have some fun! (x2)

Pupils' Interactive Activities

My Karaoke!
Entraîne-toi à chanter avec ton karaoké !

eak!

Walking down to the beach (Dorchester, England)

Re-cycle!

Remember?

Compétences
- Énumérer des activités de loisirs.
- Isoler des informations simples dans une conversation.
- Faire des suggestions d'activités.

1. Sports and leisure activities

a. Watch the slideshow. Listen and memorise the names of the activities. Video 11

b. Use the letters to write the names of the activities. Workbook p. 113

Help!

Pour parler d'une activité, tu ajoutes –**ing** au verbe d'action :
- fish → fish**ing**
- play hockey → play**ing** hockey

2. Have fun in the British Isles

Look at the map and say what activities you can do.

Example: *You can surf in Torquay, England. Surfing is so fun! I like it!*

Help!

Surfing is...
- a great experience!
- fun!
- fantastic!
- wonderful!
- brilliant!
- cool!

3. What would they like to do?

Listen to the three dialogues and complete the activities in your workbook.

Audio 76-78 | MP3 94-96 | Workbook p. 114

4. Happy campers

Look at the leaflet and guess what activities you can do at Long Lake Camp.

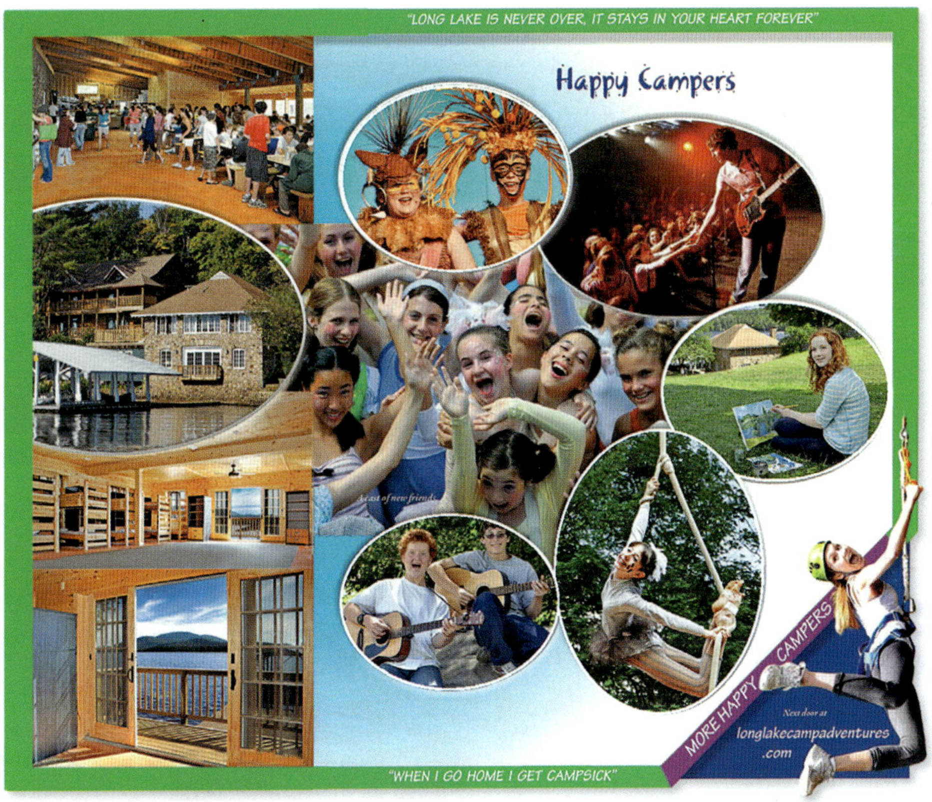

5. A weekend with your friends!

Prepare your weekend with your friends. Suggest ideas!

Lesson 1 DISCOVER
A family trip

Compétences
- Repérer des informations sur un dépliant touristique.
- Organiser une journée d'activités.
- Préparer un voyage.

1. Welcome to Holyrood Park

Workbook p. 115-116

a. What is this leaflet for?

b. Look at the leaflet and identify the different elements in your workbook.

c. Complete the wheel of activities in your workbook.

d. Find two different ways to make suggestions.

2. A day of fun in the park

Workbook p. 117

You are organising a day at Holyrood Park with your friends and your instructor. Make suggestions and complete the conversation.

3. Going on a family trip

a. Look at the people in the van: who's driving? Who are the three children? Are they all happy?

b. Look at all the objects: what do they tell you about the mother? the little boy? the two girls?

c. Imagine where they are going.

d. Your turn! What objects do you need to go on holiday?

I need my phone charger...

Extract from *Sisters*, a graphic novel by Raina Telgemeier, ©SCHOLASTIC

Compétences
- Comprendre la trame d'une bande dessinée.
- Comprendre l'essentiel des projets d'une personne.

A day out

Audio 79

1. Start the story

Workbook p. 118

From picture 1 to picture 3

a. Look at the first three pictures. React about the place, the people and the expressions on their faces.

b. Look at the entrance sign and name all the different activities.

c. In the text, find:

- The twins' opinions on the place.
- The activities each member of the family would like to do.
- The twins' reactions to their parents' suggestions. Look at their faces!

2. Imagine what happened

Workbook p. 119

Picture 4

a. Look at all the family members: do you think they all like the tree top adventure?

Find their opinions in the text.

Picture 9

b. Now look at pictures 4 and 9.
Compare the Joneses.

Example: *In picture 4 Amelia was... Now she is...*

c. Something happened! Imagine what.
Make suppositions.

3. Read the complete story

Workbook p. 120

From picture 4 to the end

a. Look at pictures 4 to 9 and read the complete comic strip. Say if your suppositions are correct or not.
Recap the classes' suggestions in your workbook.

b. In the text, find the sentence that sums up the problem.

c. Recap what happened.

4. Nosy Parker's dreams

Nosy Parker now has a video of the Jones family. Listen to him imagining his future.

a. Listen and react. Audio 80

b. Go to your workbook and take notes about Nosy Parker's future. Workbook p. 121

HAVE FUN IN GROUPS

Play "Battleship all over the world"

1. Speaking — Demander et fournir des renseignements

How to play ⏳ 10 min

Choose a place for your next holidays.

- Europe
- North America
- Africa
- Asia
- Australia
- South America

Then choose a place, accommodation and two activities you will do. Place the symbols on the map as in the example. Ask your friend questions. Guess where he or she will go and what he or she will do.

Pupil A: *Will you go to Europe? Will you ski?*

Pupil B: *Yes, I will. / No, I won't.*

Then guess exactly where: *Are you going to ski in H4?*

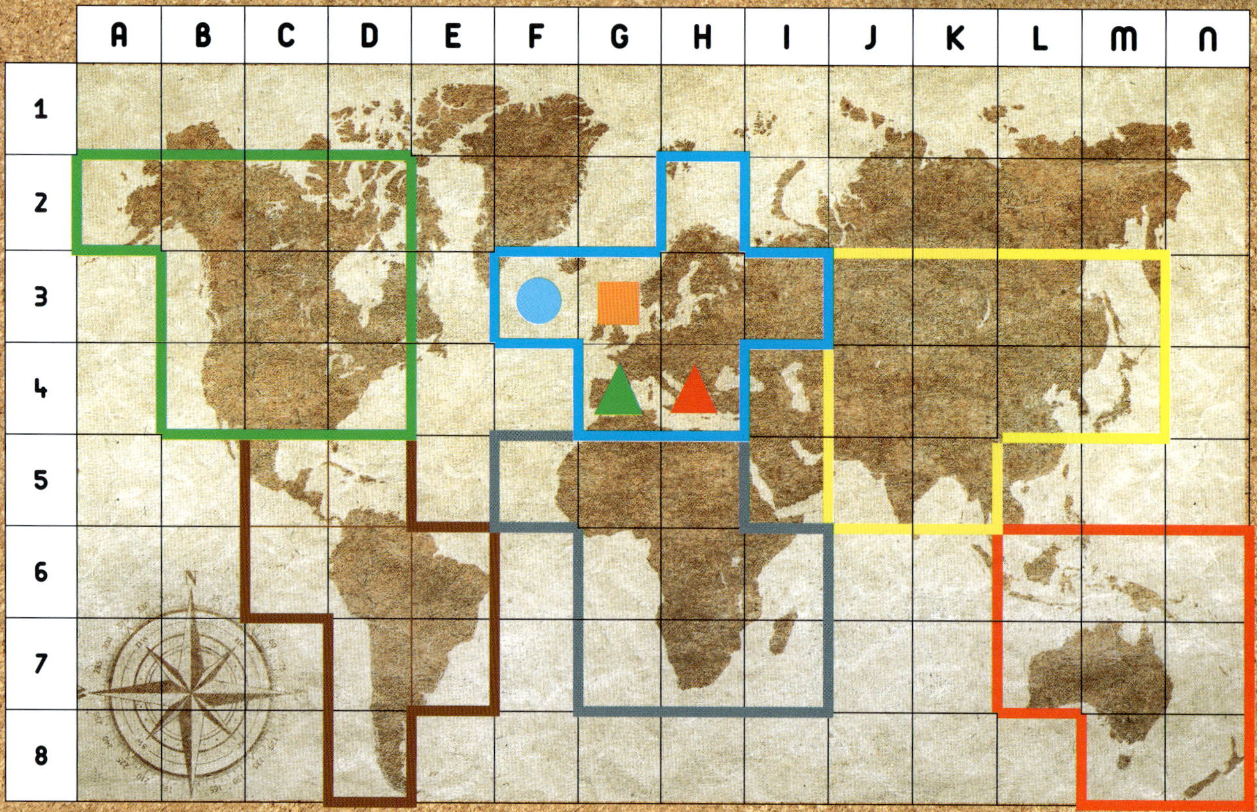

Help Yourself!

2. Listening — Comprendre l'essentiel d'un message radiophonique

→ En utilisant les indices phonologiques (intonations, etc.).
→ En prenant appui sur les images et le contexte pour anticiper le contenu.

★

MP3 97 Workbook p. 122

★★

MP3 98 Workbook p. 122

★★★

MP3 99 Workbook p. 123

Choose your document and go to your workbook for help.

3. Speaking — Lire à voix haute et de manière expressive un texte bref

→ En t'entraînant à reproduire des énoncés.
→ En modulant ta voix pour t'approprier des schémas intonatifs spécifiques.

The Duke of Edinburgh's Award

If you like adventure and competition
this race is just for you!
You like nature and you love reading maps
so what about going with your friends
on a great adventure?
You can go running, sometimes swimming,
and you can go camping. It's great fun!
But it's a race, so you must work with
your team!
It's an amazing experience! You'll love it!
Win this year's Duke of Edinburgh's Award!

Imagine you're recording a radio message.

a. Listen to the recording with your teacher.
Audio 81 MP3 100

b. Do the activities in your workbook.
Workbook p. 124

Help!

duke /juː/	**Edinburgh** /'edɪnbərə/	**award** /ə'wɔːd/
race /eɪ/	**adventure** /tʃə/	**nature** /'neɪtʃə/

Pupils' Interactive Activities
Entraîne-toi avec les exercices interactifs.

Memorise the words!

Places and activities
Pupil A suggests a place.
Pupil B associates activities.

Practise!

A La terminaison *-ing* / La consonne /ŋ/

La terminaison *-ing* est un son très nasal et très court (comme si on bloquait son souffle). La lettre « g » est muette, elle ne se prononce pas.

Listen, repeat and practise. Audio 82 MP3 101

hiking /ɪŋ/	surfing /ɪŋ/	canoeing /ɪŋ/	golfing /ɪŋ/
fishing /ɪŋ/	skiing /ɪŋ/	skating /ɪŋ/	sailing /ɪŋ/
climbing /ɪŋ/	playing /ɪŋ/	biking /ɪŋ/	swimming /ɪŋ/

B L'intonation marquant l'enthousiasme

La langue anglaise utilise beaucoup les intonations pour exprimer les sentiments. Voici quelques exemples d'intonations qui expriment l'enthousiasme.

1. Listen, repeat and practise. Audio 83 MP3 102

It's **awe**some!

It's so ex**cit**ing!

You'll have an a**maz**ing time!

2. Underline the stressed syllable, then draw the intonation. Workbook p. 125

→ Pour faire des propositions, des suggestions à quelqu'un

- **What about + V-ing + ... ?** (= action que tu proposes)
  ***What about** watch**ing** a film on TV?*
- **Why not + BV + ... ?**
  ***Why not** go to London?*
- **Let's + BV + ... !** (= pour faire quelque chose avec quelqu'un)
  ***Let's** play hockey! I love that sport.*

1 React: suggest a solution.
"We are hungry!" - "I'm tired!" - "I'm bored!"

→ Pour parler d'une action dans le futur

Will

- Forme affirmative pleine : **will + BV**
- Forme affirmative contractée : **'ll + BV**

*Tomorrow I**'ll** visit my grandparents. My grandma **will** make a cake.*

2 You'll be on holiday in July. What will you do?

Homework Workbook p. 127-128
Des exercices supplémentaires pour t'entraîner.

Workbook p. 125-126

Activities MP3 103

writing **sto**ries
/aɪ/ /ɔː/

acting
/'æktɪŋ/

singing
/ɪ/

cre**ate** **de**cors
/krɪ'eɪt/ /'deɪkɔːz/

cre**ate** **cos**tumes
/'kɒstjuːmz/

have a **camp**fire
/æ/ /aɪə/

cook **marsh**mallows
/u/ /æ/ /əʊ/

treasure hunt
/'treʒə/ /ʌ/

Places MP3 104

a lake
/eɪ/

a **for**est
/ɒ//ɪ/

mountains
/'maʊntɪnz/

a beach
/iː/

a park
/ɑː/

a camp site
/æ/ /aɪ/

a ho**tel**
/əʊ/

a spa
/ɑː/

Sports MP3 105

skating
/eɪ/

quad **bik**ing
/ɑ/ /aɪ/

climbing
/'klaɪmɪŋ/

hiking
/aɪ//ɪŋ/

playing **crick**et
/'pleɪɪŋ/ /ɪ/

playing golf
/ɒ/

playing **hock**ey
/'hɒkɪ/

playing **bas**ketball
/ɑː/ /ɪ/

playing **round**ers
/'raʊndəz/

playing **bad**minton
/æ/

ca**noe**ing
/uː/

fishing
/ɪ/

water **ski**ing
/wɔː/ /iː/

surfing
/ɜː/

sailing
/eɪ/

Final Task

Domaine 2 Socle

Come to my amazing summer camp!

Your project

Tu vas inventer un camp de vacances et réaliser une annonce publicitaire radiophonique qui en fera la présentation. Ton message devra être le plus convaincant possible !

Follow the steps

STEP 1
Design your camp!

Donne un nom à ton camp de vacances et choisis une ambiance (sportive, détente, en extérieur, artistique...). Fais la liste des activités que l'on y propose *(indoor activities, outdoor activities)*.

STEP 2
Make it sound great!

Prépare une liste d'adjectifs et d'expressions qui viendront ponctuer ton annonce et la rendre attractive et convaincante.

STEP 3
Organise your message

En introduction, adresse-toi directement à tes auditeurs pour les attirer dans ce camp de vacances *(You are.... You like..., so...)*. Fais des suggestions d'activités que l'on y propose.

STEP 4
Practise saying it

Entraîne-toi à mettre en voix ton texte : tu dois donner l'impression qu'il s'agit d'un message publicitaire. N'écris pas tout, essaie de mémoriser.

STEP 5
You're online!

Option 1 : Enregistre ton message.

Option 2 : Viens faire ta présentation devant le reste de la classe.

I BET YOU CAN!

MAINTENANT, TU ES CAPABLE DE :

- Isoler des informations simples dans une conversation (sur les loisirs). A1
- Identifier le sujet d'un message radiophonique. A1
- Lire à haute voix et de manière expressive. A1
- Réagir à des propositions et donner ton avis. A1
- échanger des renseignements sur des projets futurs. A1
- Repérer des informations ciblées sur un document informatif. A1
- Faire une brève annonce publicitaire. A2

Ton/ta professeur(e) te distribuera des fiches pour t'évaluer.

N'oublie pas d'utiliser :

- le lexique des sports (p. 126, 135)
- le lexique des activités (p. 135)
- l'expression des goûts (p. 67)
- l'expression de la capacité (p. 67)
- les suggestions (p. 134)
- la prononciation des exclamations et l'intonation de l'enthousiasme (p. 134)

Tu veux t'améliorer ?

Rends-toi page 173 à la **Banque d'exercices** et entraîne-toi à utiliser :

- *Will* + BV
- Les suggestions
- Le lexique de l'unité

UNIT 8

Legends and

DANS CETTE UNITÉ

Tu vas découvrir

- Des héros / héroïnes de contes et de films
- La légende de Merlin et Arthur
- L'épilogue des aventures de la famille Jones

Tu vas apprendre à

- Suivre le fil d'une histoire
- Décrire un héros ou une héroïne
- Comprendre une légende
- Produire quelques phrases sur un personnage imaginaire
- Comprendre le contenu d'un article
- Imaginer une histoire

Et tu vas

Final Task ▸ Imaginer ce qui se passe dans le dernier épisode du Story Time

Rhyme Time

Audio 84

MP3 106

Here come the fairytales

Here come the fairies, here come the witches.
Here come the giants, and trolls from the ditches.

Here's Sleeping Beauty, a prince and a king.
A wicked stepmother, a spell and a ring.

Out of the storybooks, falling from pages,
Stories of magic and tales through the ages. [...]

By Brenda Williams

Tales

Eilean Donan Castle, Scotland

Re-cycle!

Remember?

Compétences
- Acquérir le lexique des contes et légendes.
- Suivre le fil d'une histoire.
- Décrire un héros ou une héroïne.

1. Storytelling

a. Look at the mindmap. Listen and repeat the vocabulary of fairy tales. Audio 85

b. Read the sentences and find the corresponding stories. Workbook p. 129

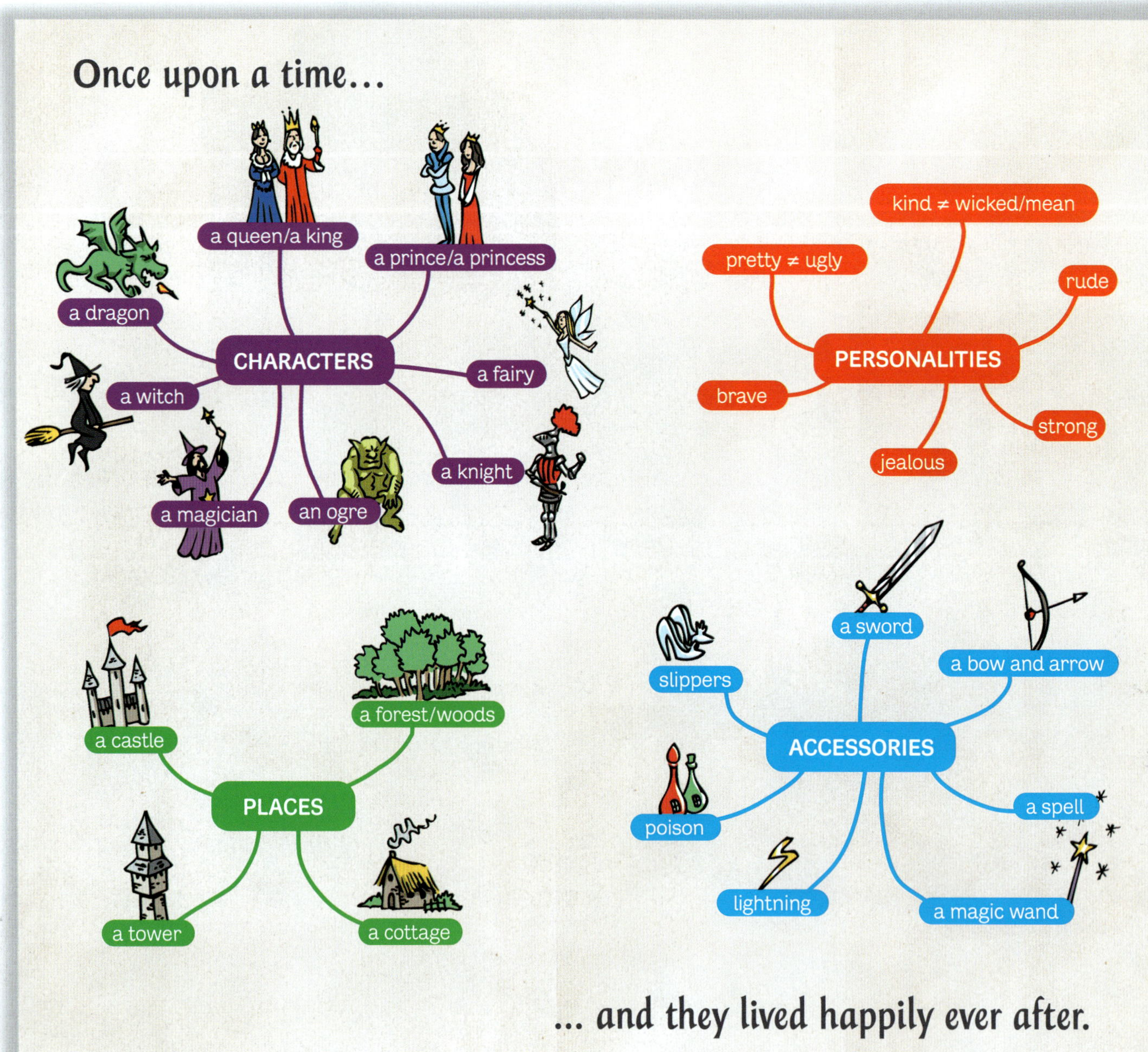

2. Stories turned into films

a. Look at the posters, choose a character and describe him/her (clothes/physical description).

b. Go to your workbook and solve the riddles. Workbook p. 130

3. My favourite hero! Audio 86

Listen and identify who they are talking about.
Why do they like them?

Tom likes ... because...

4. Express yourself!

Express your opinion about a character of your choice!

"Brave" is my favourite character because ...

Lesson 1 DISCOVER
A legend

Compétences
- Comprendre une légende.
- Produire quelques phrases sur un personnage imaginaire.

1. Enter the legend! Workbook p. 131-132

a. Look at the title: there are two names. Read the first paragraph. Find information about these two characters.

b. Read the text: what words do you recognize?

c. Build a mindmap to classify the different elements from the tale (use the model p. 140).

d. Reorder the pictures to match the story.

The legend of Arthur and Merlin

Once upon a time, in an enchanted forest there was an old magician named Merlin. He lived in an old tower. One day, he heard a baby boy crying in front of the tower. Merlin sensed that he was special, and he said:

"Your name will be Arthur and one day you will be king!"

Merlin gave Arthur to his friends, the brave knight Sir Hector and his son named Kay. Merlin visited Arthur every day to give him lessons. But Arthur preferred fighting with Kay.

One day, Kay went to fight at a great tournament. Arthur was his page but he forgot Kay's sword! In the woods, Arthur saw a big stone with a sword in it. Quickly, he pulled out the sword. It was easy! Sir Hector and Kay were very surprised.

"That's impossible!" cried Sir Hector, "that sword is Excalibur". There was a message on the stone:

WHOEVER SHALL REMOVE THIS SWORD*
FROM THE STONE
IS THE NEW KING OF BRITAIN.

Sir Hector panicked: "Arthur, you must replace it immediately!" So Arthur replaced the sword.

Later that day, after the tournament, the other knights wanted to take the sword too, but it was impossible. Merlin declared:

"Let Arthur take the sword".

They all mocked Arthur because he was just a small boy. But Arthur walked to the stone and pulled it out again!

He was proclaimed the new King of Britain and all the knights shouted:

"Long live our new
King Arthur!"

* *Quiconque retirera cette épée...*

2. The sword in the stone

Look at the picture. What part of the text does it correspond to?

3. The legend of Aurora

Workbook p. 133-135

Discover the document

Look at the document and do the activities in your workbook.

Writing time

Write *your* version of the legend of Aurora.

Lesson 2 Story TIME

Compétences
- Comprendre le contenu d'un article.
- Imaginer une histoire.

1. Aliens in Liverpool

a. Say what you remember about the Jones family and their weekend at the park (see p. 130).

b. Complete the following sentences. *This is an article from... It's an article about...*

c. Go to your workbook and check what you understand. Workbook p. 136-137

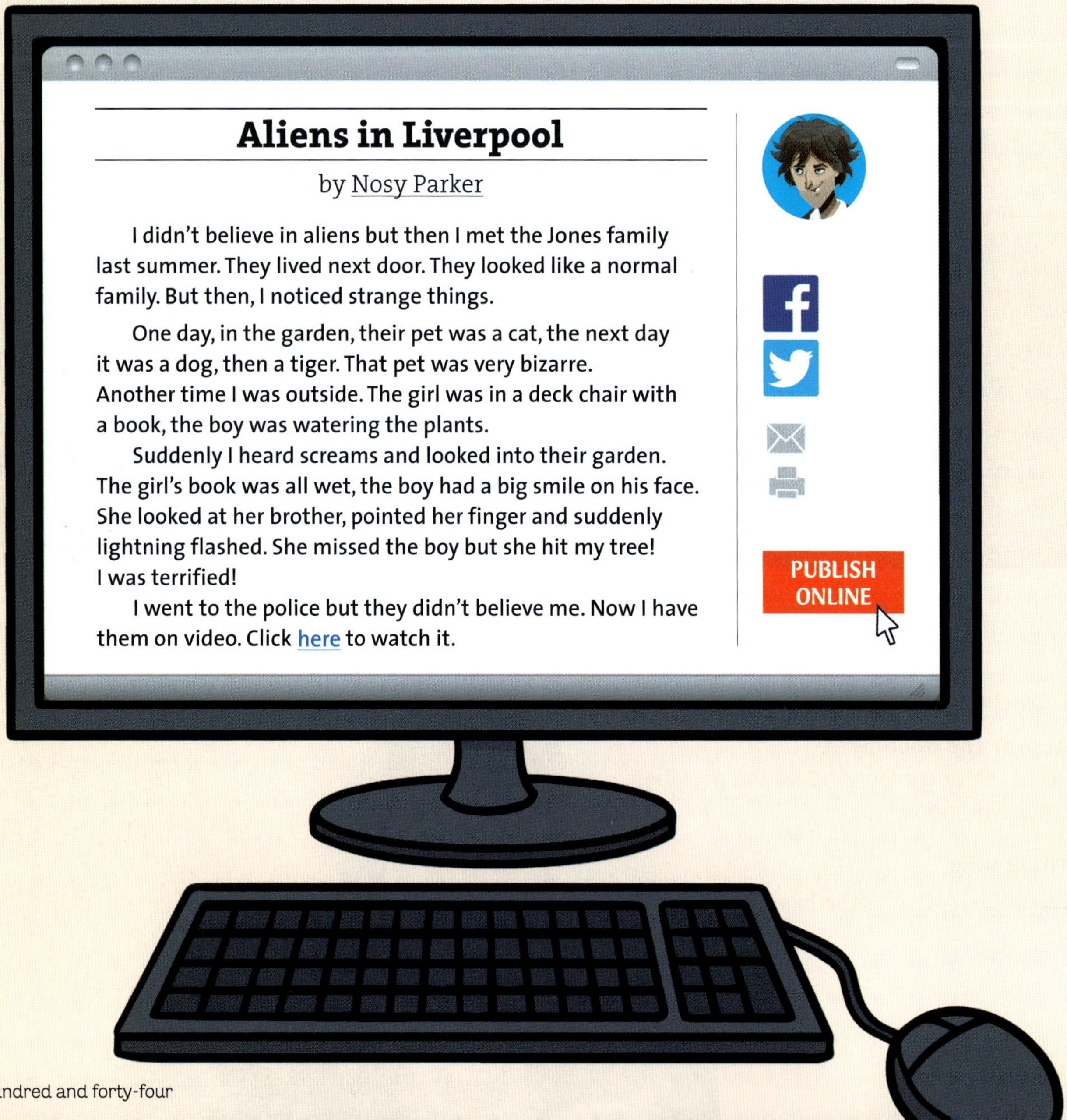

Aliens in Liverpool

by Nosy Parker

I didn't believe in aliens but then I met the Jones family last summer. They lived next door. They looked like a normal family. But then, I noticed strange things.

One day, in the garden, their pet was a cat, the next day it was a dog, then a tiger. That pet was very bizarre. Another time I was outside. The girl was in a deck chair with a book, the boy was watering the plants.

Suddenly I heard screams and looked into their garden. The girl's book was all wet, the boy had a big smile on his face. She looked at her brother, pointed her finger and suddenly lightning flashed. She missed the boy but she hit my tree! I was terrified!

I went to the police but they didn't believe me. Now I have them on video. Click here to watch it.

2. Imagine "The Grand Finale" — Final Task

Vous allez être les scénaristes du dernier épisode de la saison 1.

- Nosy Parker s'apprête à publier son article qui révèle les pouvoirs particuliers de la famille Jones.
À vous d'imaginer la fin et de la partager avec la classe.
Voici comment débuter le récit : *After the trip to the park, Nosy Parker went home and typed his article on his computer...*
- Une fois votre version corrigée par ton/ta professeur(e), tu peux la mettre en images sous la forme d'un storyboard.

Regardez ensuite la version imaginée par les auteurs. Aviez-vous pensé à cela?

N'oublie pas !
Tu vas rédiger ton histoire au prétérit, et utiliser des verbes réguliers et irréguliers. Rappelle-toi des règles (voir p. 121 et p. 146).

The Grand Finale

Video 12

Pupils' Interactive Activities
Entraîne-toi avec les exercices interactifs.

Memorise the words!

Characters, accessories and places
Pupil A names a character.
Pupil B says:
- who he/she is
- how he/she is
- what he/she has got
- where he/she lives.

Practise!

La mise en voix d'un texte
Listen to first paragraph of the legend of Merlin and repeat in the same way.

Audio 87 | MP3 107 | Workbook p. 138

*Once u**pon** a time, // in an en**chan**ted **for**est //*
/ɪd/
*there was an old ma**gi**cian named **Mer**lin. //*
He lived in an old tower. // One day, he heard
/d/
*a **ba**by boy crying in front of the tower. // **Mer**lin*
*sensed that he was **spe**cial, // and he said:*
/t/
*"Your name will be **Ar**thur // and one day //*
you will be king!"

→ *Pour écrire un récit au passé*

Le prétérit

Fais attention aux verbes irréguliers, c'est-à-dire ceux qui ne suivent pas la règle de la terminaison ***-ed.***

1 Can you correct these tales or legends?
a. Little Red Riding Hood lived with her grandmother. She was a princess.
b. Cinderella had two brothers. She didn't go to the Prince's ball.
c. Merlin was a king. He had a son. Arthur did not pull the sword out of the stone.
d. Shrek didn't like Fiona.

→ *Pour structurer un récit*

Les marqueurs de temps

Emploie-les pour indiquer le **déroulement chronologique** : *one day / once upon a time / at first / then...*

Les mots de liaison

Emploie-les pour **relier des phrases** : *and* (addition), *but* (opposition), *because* (cause), *so* (conséquence).

2 Complete this legend.
(...) there was a very disobedient girl. (...) she decided to visit the old witch in the forest (...) her mother refused. (...) the girl went out at night (...) walked to the witch's cottage. The old witch appeared (...) said: "You are trembling (...) you're cold." (...) "Come in, I'll make a fire." (...) she changed the girl into a block of wood.

Homework Workbook p. 140-141
Des exercices supplémentaires pour t'entraîner.

Characters MP3 108

- a **fair**y /eə/
- a prince and a prin**cess** /ɪ/ /ɪ/ /e/
- a king and a queen /ɪ/ /iː/
- a witch /ɪ/
- a ma**gi**cian /məˈdʒɪʃən/
- an **o**gre /əʊ/
- elves /elvz/
- a knight /naɪt/
- a **Vi**king **war**rior /aɪ/ /ɒ/

Animals and creatures MP3 111

- a **wolf**-dog /ʊ/
- a wolf /ʊ/
- a **were**wolf /ɪə/
- a **don**key /ˈdɒŋki/
- a beast /iː/
- a **drag**on /æ/
- a bear /eə/
- a **li**on /aɪə/
- a **ti**ger /aɪ/

Personality MP3 109

- kind /aɪ/
- mean /iː/
- **grum**py /ʌ/ /i/
- rude /uː/
- **hand**some /ˈhænsəm/
- **pre**tty /ɪ/ /i/
- brave /eɪ/

Accessories MP3 112

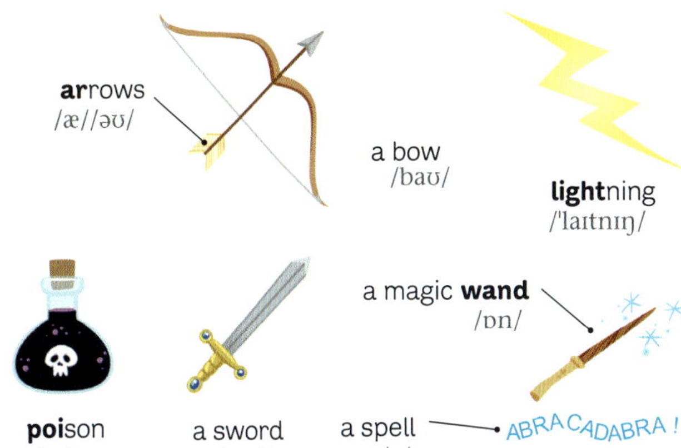

- **ar**rows /æ/ /əʊ/
- a bow /baʊ/
- **light**ning /ˈlaɪtnɪŋ/
- **poi**son /ɔɪ/
- a sword /sɔːd/
- a magic **wand** /ɒn/
- a spell /e/

Places MP3 110

- a **cas**tle /ɑː/
- a **cot**tage /kɒtɪdʒ/
- a cave /eɪ/

I BET YOU CAN!

Ton/ta professeur(e) te distribuera des fiches pour t'évaluer.

Tu veux t'améliorer ?

Rends-toi p. 174 à la **Banque d'exercices**

et entraîne-toi à utiliser :

- Le prétérit
- Les marqueurs de temps
- Le lexique de l'unité

Sommaire des annexes

October
31

Halloween decorations in London

Carving a pumpkin to create a Jack-o-lantern

HALLOWEEN

TRADITIONS & THEIR ORIGINS

Halloween is celebrated on **October 31st** in the United Kingdom, the United States, and other English-speaking countries like Canada and Ireland. It is a very old Celtic festival (2,000 years old) to "scare the ghosts and the spirits". Today, Halloween is a fun day for children. Jack-o-lanterns, spiders and spooky monsters are famous symbols of this celebration.

Children dress up in scary costumes. They go from door to door and say "Trick or treat?" to have candies.

DO IT YOURSELF!

Pumpkin Pie Recipe

You can cook special food on Halloween, like a pumpkin pie.

1. Carve out a pumpkin and cook the pulp.
2. Add cream and sugar.
3. Spread on pre-made pastry.
4. Cook in the oven for 40 minutes. Yummy!

LET'S SING AND RAP!

Audio 88
MP3 113

Pumpkin, pumpkin,
Round and fat,
Turn into a Jack-o-lantern,
Just like that!

Story TIME

Halloween Special Episode

It's Halloween tonight and Amelia, Oliver and their friends are going trick-or-treating from door to door. Let's follow them!

Video 13

a. Can you name the characters?

b. Where are they? In a garden? In a cemetery? In a park?

c. Can you name 5 objects related to Halloween?

CELEBRATE WITH A POEM!

In a dark, dark wood, there was a dark, dark house.
And in the dark, dark house, there was a dark, dark room.
And in the dark, dark room, there was a dark, dark cupboard.
And in the dark, dark cupboard, there was a dark, dark shelf.
And on the dark, dark shelf, there was a dark, dark box.
And in the dark, dark box,
*There was a ... **ghost!***

Get ready to learn the poem by heart!

a. Which adjective is repeated?

b. Make a list of the 7 nouns used in the poem and memorise them.

c. Now read it slowly and insist on the repeated adjective: what effect is created?

d. When saying the last verse what can you do?

November
5

Fireworks

A puppet of Guy Fawkes (after his arrest)

GUY FAWKES NIGHT
Bonfire Night

TRADITIONS & THEIR ORIGINS

On November 5th 1605, a Catholic man called Guy Fawkes tried to blow up the English Parliament to kill the Protestant King James I because he wasn't happy with the King's decisions. He was arrested and hanged.
Every **November 5th,** the English celebrate the capture of Guy Fawkes and the King's survival! They make puppets of Guy Fawkes and burn them on a bonfire. And then, they watch fireworks.

A bonfire

LET'S CHANT! Audio 89 MP3 114

Remember, remember the fifth of November
Gunpowder, treason and plot*.
[I see] no reason why gunpowder treason
Should ever be forgot.

* *complot*

DO IT YOURSELF!

Make a mini Guy Fawkes

Your teacher will give you the link to type in your browser. Go to this website and follow the "photo steps".

Story TIME
Christmas Special Episode

CHRISTMAS

Christmas time! What are the twins dreaming of?
How are they celebrating Christmas?

Video 14

a. Where are the characters?

b. What time of the year is it? How can you tell?

c. How many tree decorations can you see?

LET'S SING! Audio 90 MP3 115

WE WISH YOU A MERRY CHRISTMAS

We wish you a Merry Christmas! (x2)
We wish you a Merry Christmas
And a Happy New Year!
Good tidings we bring to you and your kin
We wish you a Merry Christmas
and a Happy New Year!

Oh, bring us a figgy pudding, (x2)
Oh, bring us a figgy pudding
And a cup of good cheer!

We won't go until we get some, (x2)
We won't go until we get some,
So bring some out here!

We wish you a Merry Christmas! (x2)
We wish you a Merry Christmas
And a Happy New Year

December
24-25

Christmas trees are decorated with balls and tinsel.

TRADITIONS & THEIR ORIGINS

It is a religious holiday and a cultural phenomenon! Celebrated on **December 25th,** it's a time of joy with family and friends.
People love decorating their houses.
British and American people love sending Christmas cards, and they decorate their living rooms with the cards they receive from friends or family.
Sending Christmas cards is a very old tradition in English-speaking countries. The first cards were created in London in 1843.

Christmas stockings

Christmas stockings and Christmas cards on the fireplace

On Christmas Eve, on December 24th, children get very excited and wait for **Santa Claus** to come with presents.

CELEBRATE WITH A POEM!

Audio 93 MP3 118

Read these lines aloud, and emphasise the underlined syllables. Can you hear the rhythm? Now memorise it!

Little Jack Horner
Sat in the corner,
Eating a Christmas pie;
He put in his thumb,
And took out a plum,
And said, "What a good boy am I!

Norman Rockwell,
Santa Claus and "Tommy's drum"
(1951)

Pulling crackers

DO IT YOURSELF!

You can create your Christmas Crackers!

At Christmas dinner, people have fun with "Christmas crackers", displayed on the table. You pull the cracker with your neighbour and it opens with a "bang". You get little presents like paper hats...

You need: a cardboard roll, paper, ribbons and a glue stick.

1. Cut the cardboard roll.
2. Put a small gift or a personal message inside!
3. Put paper around.
4. Tie ribbons at each end.

Your teacher will give you the link to type in your browser. Just follow the steps!

Do you know?

Father Christmas's reindeers are called Rudolf, Dasher, Dancer, Prancer, Vixen, Comet, Cupid, Donner and Blitzen. Rudolf is the leader because its red nose is a light in the dark.

Decorations in Covent Garden, London

March 17

St Patrick's Day in Dublin

People put green clothes on and leprechaun hats. People also wear shamrocks, the emblem of Ireland.

SAINT PATRICK'S DAY

A leprechaun

TRADITIONS & THEIR ORIGINS

Saint Patrick's Day is a cultural and religious celebration.
On **March 17th**, Irish people, all around the world, celebrate Saint Patrick (AD 385-461), the patron saint of Ireland.

Green, green, green, at St Patrick's Parade!

LET'S SING AND DANCE!

Audio 91 MP3 116

I'm a little leprechaun, *(hands on hips)*
Dressed in green, *(point to shirt)*
The tiniest man *(hold thumb and index finger about an inch apart)*
That you have seen.
(point to the other people)
If you ever catch me, so it's told,
(make a motion like you're grabbing at a leprechaun)
I'll give you my big pot of gold.
(make a motion like you're giving something away)

DO IT YOURSELF!

Make a leprechaun hat

Your teacher will give you the link to type in your browser. Print the pattern and follow the steps! It's very easy!

EASTER

TRADITIONS & THEIR ORIGINS

Easter is a religious celebration. The **"Easter Bunny"** is an Easter symbol. The bunny (= rabbit) brings and hides chocolate eggs in the garden. This tradition is of German origin. On Easter Sunday, children look for the eggs and play outside.

In the USA, this celebration is very important, especially at the White House! The **White House Easter Egg Roll** is a very old and unique tradition.

The Easter Bunny with Michelle and Barack Obama

DO IT YOURSELF!

Hot cross buns

A **hot cross bun** is a sweet bun traditionally eaten in English-speaking countries. People eat them on Good Friday. Your teacher will give you the link to the recipe to type in your browser. Follow **Jamie Oliver's recipe** and make delicious buns.

The **Easter Parade** is an old tradition dating back to 1870. On **Easter Sunday,** in New York and other American cities, people wear new clothes and **extraordinary hats**. Some competitions are organised: the best Easter hat wins a prize.

LET'S SING!

Audio 92
MP3 117

Hot cross buns!
Hot cross buns!
One a penny, two a penny,
Hot cross buns!
Give them to your daughters,
Give them to your sons.
One a penny, two a penny,
Hot cross buns!

MEET THE ARTISTS WHO HAVE INFLUENCED...

Musical Legends

...THE SONGS OF I BET YOU CAN!

MP3 20 **"How are you today?"**

is inspired by

The Beatles

The Beatles are a legendary rock band formed in Liverpool in 1960. They composed very famous songs like ***"Yesterday"***, ***"Hello, Goodbye"***, ***"Yellow Submarine"*** or ***"Let it Be"***. Their nickname is "The Fab Four" because there were four of them and they were fabulous! The Beatles are: John Lennon, Paul McCartney, George Harrison and Ringo Starr. They sold over 600 million records and their music has influenced a lot of artists. They even received a medal from Queen Elizabeth II.

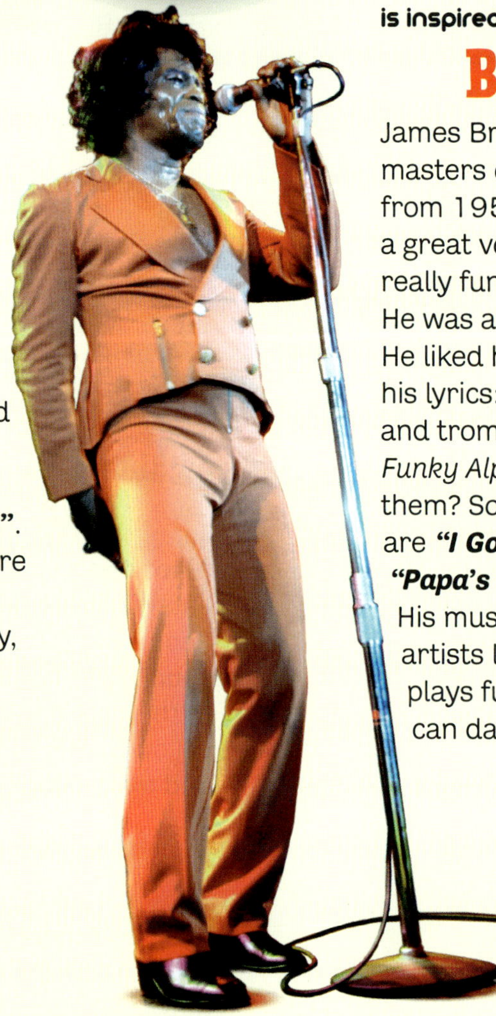

MP3 02 **"The Funky Alphabet"**

is inspired by

James Brown

James Brown was one of the masters of funk and soul music from 1956 to 2006. He had a great voice and his music is really funky with a lot of rhythm. He was an excellent dancer too! He liked horns to accompany his lyrics: saxophones, trumpets and trombones! Listen to "*The Funky Alphabet*", can you hear them? Some of his famous hits are ***"I Got You (I Feel Good)"*** or ***"Papa's Got a Brand New Bag"***. His music influenced a lot of artists like Bruno Mars who plays funky music and who can dance too!

MP3 81 **"Let's go to London!"**

is inspired by

The Clash

The Clash is an English punk rock band formed in 1976 with Joe Strummer as the leader. They lived in Camden Town, London, and their most famous album is called ***"London Calling"***. They played rock music but also reggae and ska! Everybody knows the song ***"Should I Stay or Should I Go"***.

MP3 41

"Family" is inspired by the Red Hot Chili Peppers

The Red Hot Chili Peppers are an American band formed in Los Angeles in 1983. Their music genre is unique and mixes rock, rap and funk!
They composed popular songs such as ***"Under the Bridge"***, ***"By the Way"*** or ***"Aeroplane"***.

MP3 69

"Happy birthday" is inspired by Gwen Stefani

Gwen Stefani is an American singer and fashion designer. She was born in 1969. She was the lead singer of the ska pop band No Doubt which was one of the most famous ska bands in the 2000s, with their hit song ***"Hey Baby"*** and their album ***"Rock Steady"***. In 2004, she started a solo career. She won 3 Grammy Awards and was on the "100 Greatest Women in Music" list in 2012. She has sold more than 30 million albums worldwide.

MP3 93

"Let's have some fun!" is inspired by Green Day

Green Day is an American punk rock band formed in 1986 in California. They are a trio: guitar, bass and drums. Green Day has sold more than 85 million records worldwide and has won five Grammy Awards. They play fast music with nice melodies which are easy to remember! Their famous hits are ***"Basket Case"*** and ***"American Idiot'.*** Artists like Avril Lavigne or Pink have been influenced by their music!

TEST YOURSELF!

How much do you know about these musicians?

1. Who were the Fab Four?

2. Where were they from?

3. What kind of music did James Brown sing?

4. What special instruments did James Brown use?

5. Where did the Clash live?

6. What kind of music did the Clash play?

7. She is an American singer and fashion designer.

8. Give the title of a famous album by the Clash.

9. What genres of music do the Red Hot Chili Peppers mix?

10. How many people are there in Green Day?

Answers: 1. The Beatles **2.** Liverpool, England **3.** Funk and soul music **4.** Horns (saxophones, trumpets and trombones) **5.** In Camden Town, London **6.** Punk rock, rock music, reggae, ska **7.** Gwen Stefani **8.** *London Calling* **9.** Rock, rap and funk **10.** Three

CLASS ACTIVITY

THE BLIND TEST GAME!

Get into groups.
Listen to the songs your teacher is playing and try to guess the band!

Great Britain Through the Ages

WHO RULED GREAT BRITAIN?

1 Boudicca
-61 BC

2 Emperor Claudius
41 – 54 AD

3 Alfred the Great
878 – 899

4 William the Conqueror
1066 – 1087

WHAT DID THEY DO?

± 750 BC
Celtic Britain
The Celts invaded Britain and adopted some ancient traditions.

43 to 410 AD
Roman Britain
The Romans called London 'Londonium'. They built forts, roads, and Roman baths.

410 to 1066
Anglo-Saxon Britain
The Vikings from Scandinavia invaded Great Britain and founded the city of York.

1066 to 1154
The Norman Conquest
They built a lot of castles to control the country.

TODAY, WE CAN SEE...

Castell Henllys (Wales)

Roman baths in Bath

a Viking helmet (The British Museum)

The Tower of London

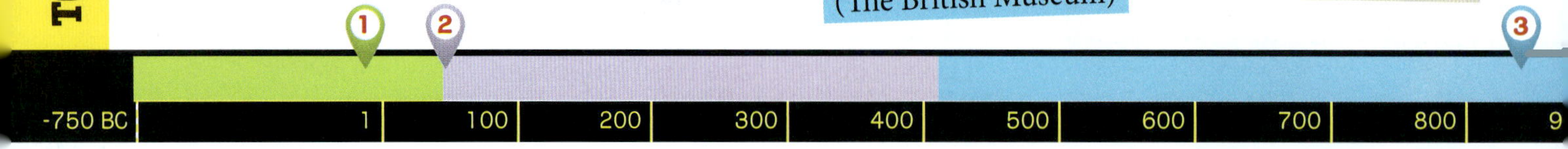

1154 to 1485

The Plantagenets

They fought France from 1337 to 1453 in the Hundred Years' War.

1485 to 1603

The Tudors

They loved the arts, built theatres and supported Shakespeare's plays.

1714 to 1901

Georgian & Victorian Britain

They fought and defeated Napoleon at the Battle of Trafalgar.

MODERN TIMES

Modern Elizabethan Britain

After 47 years, the UK left the European Union on December 31st 2020. This departure is known as Brexit.

Winchester and the Round Table

Hampton Court Palace

The British Rail system

The Millennium Bridge

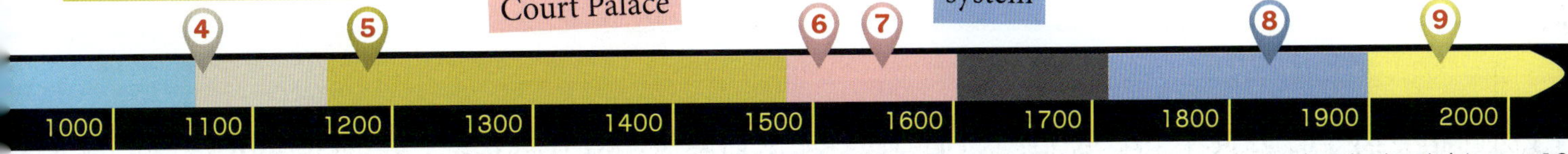

WHO GOVERNED THE USA?

WHAT DID THEY DO?

1789-1797

American Independence

The 13 Colonies declared independence from England on July 4th, 1776. The Constitution was adopted in 1788.

1861-1865

The Civil War

This war opposed the Confederacy and the Union. President Lincoln abolished slavery at the end of the war.

1901-1909

The Progressive Era

He created nature reserves to protect wildlife and the environment. Mass-produced cars appeared.

1933-1945

The New Deal

The government created jobs and social security after the Great Depression. The USA fought in World War II.

1961-(1963)-1969

The Civil Rights Movement

JFK was assassinated in 1963. LBJ signed the Civil Rights Act into law, banning discrimination.

ICONIC SYMBOLS

The Liberty Bell symbolises American independence.

Union and Confederate soldiers fighting at the Battle of Franklin.

Ford's Model T was the first mass-produced car.

American soldiers landing in Normandy, France on "D-Day" in 1944.

Rosa Parks was a civil rights activist in Montgomery, Alabama.

1 2 3

17th - 18th centuries | 19th century

1969-1974

The Nixon Era

The first man landed on the moon and scientists created the Internet. (But the Web as we know it was born in the 1990s).

1981-1989

The Reagan Era

He was a former Hollywood actor and presided over the end of the Cold War.

2009-2017

The Obama Era

He was the first Black president of the United States. The use of social media and smartphones boomed!

2017-2021

The Trump Years

He is the first president to have been impeached twice.

2021-?

The Biden Presidency

He nominated the first gender-balanced and first majority non-white Cabinet. He intends to deal with the climate change issue.

Neil Armstrong walked on the moon on July 20th, 1969.

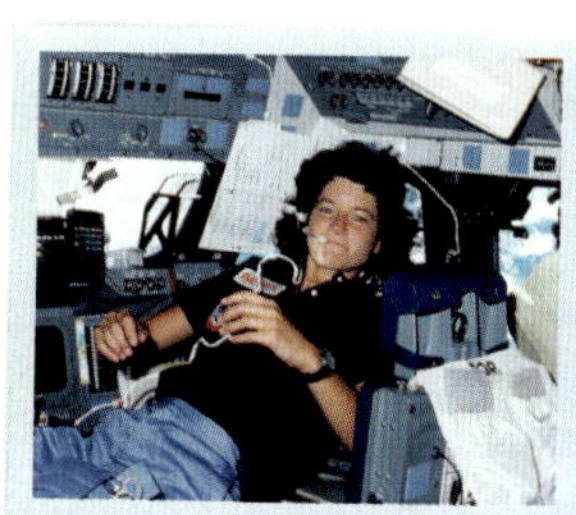

Sally Ride became the first American woman in space in 1983.

Mark Zuckerberg founded Facebook in the 2000s. Today it has more than 1.7 billion users.

Hillary Clinton was the first female Democratic presidential nominee.

Kamala Harris is the first woman and the first person of colour to become Vice President.

Exercise Bank

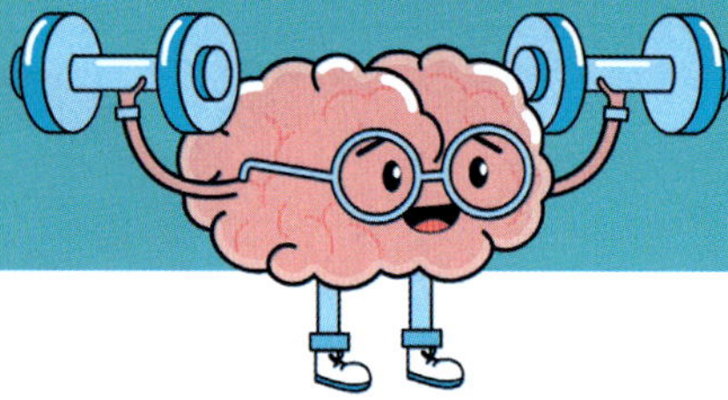

UNIT 1 (pp. 16-33)

GRAMMAIRE

Be • Les pronoms personnels sujets • Les mots interrogatifs

1 Complète les phrases avec *be* à la forme affirmative et négative.

Ex. : *Amelia **is** a supporter of Liverpool football club, she **isn't** a supporter of Manchester United.*

a. Richie ... my best friend, but he ... in my school.
b. Arsenal and Chelsea ... football clubs, they ... rugby clubs.
c. I ... in year 7, I ... in year 8.
d. The flag for England ... white and red, it ... white and red and blue.
e. You ... very funny but you ... silly!
f. Sports cars ... very fast but they ... very comfortable.
g. Ireland ... beautiful but it ... very sunny.

2 Complète les courts dialogues avec la bonne forme de *be*.

a. – ... you French? – Yes, I ....
b. – ... Amelia 11 years old? – Yes, she ...
c. – ... cats and dogs good friends? – No, they ...
d. – ... Prince Harry American? – No, he ...
e. – ... the White House in Washington, D.C.? – Yes, it ...
f. – ... we in a big school? – Yes, we ...
g. – ... we on holiday? – No, we ...
h. – ... you from Australia? – No, I ...
i. – ... the Australian flag white, blue and red? – Yes, it ...

3 Complète avec le pronom personnel qui convient.

a. Ariana is from Florida, ... is a great singer!
b. Josh is from Scotland, ... is a very nice boy.
c. Agatha Christie is an English writer, ... is very famous.
d. Sherlock Holmes and Watson are detectives, ... are friends.
e. *Robinson Crusoe* is a good book, ... is very famous.
f. My brother and my sister are 14, ... are twins.
g. This flag is for Ireland: ... is green, white and orange.
h. Amelia is British, ... is from Liverpool.

4 Complète ces réponses sur le modèle de l'exemple.

Ex. : *Is Amelia from England? Yes, she is.*

a. – Is Drake from the USA? – Yes, ...
b. – Is Maya from Ireland? – Yes, ...
c. – Is Enola Holmes an adult? – No, ...
d. – Are Imagine Dragons from Las Vegas? – Yes, ...
e. – Are the Joneses from London? – No, ...
f. – Are you a teacher? – No, ...
g. – Are you a school kid? – Yes, ...
h. – Is the exercise finished? – Yes, ...

5 Complète les questions avec le mot interrogatif qui convient.

a. – ... old are the twins? – They are 11 years old.
b. – ... is New York City? – It's in America.
c. – ...'s your favourite colour? – It's blue.
d. – ...'s the name of this cute black and white dog? – Snoopy.
e. – ... is your English teacher? – He / She is in the English classroom.
f. – ... old is your baby sister? – She is just 10 months old.

6 Remets les mots dans l'ordre pour former des phrases.

a. British - is - American - Ed Sheeran - is - not - he
b. she - singer - is - Adele - from - a - is - London
c. not - he - is - John - is - brother - sporty - my
d. they - Manchester - Are - from - ?
e. name - is – What - your - family - ?
f. Ireland - capital - is - of - Dublin - the

LEXIQUE
La famille • Les actions • La personnalité

7 Bart Simpson présente sa famille. Complète les phrases avec les mots appropriés.

My ... is Bart and my ... is Simpson. I'm ... the USA. My ... is Marge and my ... is Homer. My ... are Maggie and Lisa. We are a ... (≠ normal) and ... (= comic) family.

8 Joue à l'interprète. Peux-tu traduire les éléments manquants ?

a.	my brother	...
b.	...	ma famille
c.	...	des enfants
d.	twins	...
e.	...	jaune
f.	pink	...
g.	silly	...
h.	...	mon adresse
i.	Wales	...
j.	...	Écosse

9 Que te demande-t-on de faire le plus souvent en classe ? Retrouve le plus d'actions possibles et écris-les.
Ex. : *Listen*

UNIT 2 (pp. 34-51)

GRAMMAIRE
Have got • Can / Can't

10 En France, tu n'as pas d'uniforme : indique ce que tu ne portes donc pas, puis ce que tu as en commun avec l'uniforme des écoles anglaises.

a. I haven't got a blazer and ...
b. But I've got ...

11 Complète ces réponses avec *be* ou *have got*.

a. Has Amelia got brown hair? Yes, ...
b. Has Oliver got brown hair? No, ...
c. Are the twins from Liverpool? Yes, ...
d. Is Mr. Jones sporty? Yes, ...
e. Have they got a pet? Yes, ...
f. Are they American? No, ...

12 Réécris les questions en mettant les mots dans l'ordre, puis réponds-y.

a. you - got - schoolbag - Have - your - ?
b. a brick house - got - Shonny - Has - ?
c. on Monday - Have - got - your friends - double PE - ?
d. a lot of tests - got - we - Have - this week - ?
e. Oliver - got - short red hair - Has - ?
f. A uniform - Have - Amelia and Oliver - got - ?

13 Change la forme du verbe pour que le contenu corresponde à la réalité.
Ex. : *Shonny **has got** a horrible garden. → Shonny **hasn't got** a horrible garden.*

a. Shonny hasn't got a uniform.
b. She has got a pink and red tie.
c. She is American.
d. She hasn't got a blazer.
e. She has got a blue shirt.
f. Shonny is 20 years old.

14 **Complète ces phrases, soit avec une forme de *Be* (*am* / *is* / *are*) soit avec *has* / *have got*.**

Sherlock Holmes ... a detective. He ...British. He ... a house in London. He ... a partner, Dr Watson. They ... very good friends. But they ... a lot of enemies!

15 **Écris 2 phrases pour dire les matières que tu aimes et celles que tu n'aimes pas. Utilise *and* et *but*, comme dans l'exemple.**

Ex. : *I like French **and** I like history **but** I don't like PE **and** I don't like music.*

16 **Complète le règlement avec *can* si l'activité est autorisée ou avec *can't* si elle est interdite.**

a. You can talk with your friends in the playground but you can't use your mobile.
b. You can't be late and you can't run in the corridors.
c. In the school library, you can read comics but you can't eat chewing gum.
d. In the drama hall, you can look at the costumes but you can't touch them.
e. In the playground, you can have fun with your friends but you can't fight.
f. You can't watch videos on your mobile but you can watch them in the school library.

LEXIQUE
L'école (lieux, uniforme, objets scolaires)

17 **Retrouve de quel lieu d'une école il est question dans ces phrases.**

a. We can do PE in the ... and play football or rugby on the ... .
b. Lunch is in the ... . At break time we are in the ... .
c. We can read books and comics or use computers in the ... .
d. We do science in the ... .
e. We have French or Spanish or German or Italian in the language ... .

18 **Décris ton école britannique imaginaire. Complète les phrases suivantes.**

In my school, there's a ... and ... for PE, a ... for physics, a ... for lunch and a ... for break time. There are lots of books and magazines in the ....

19 **Complète la description d'Amelia Jones.**

Amelia is a British schoolgirl so she has got a ... . She has got a ... (1) but she hasn't got .... She has got a ... (2) and a ... . For PE, she has got ... (3) and ... and a ... (4) .

20 **Retrouve le plus d'objets possibles que peut contenir ton cartable.**

UNIT 3 (pp. 52-69)

GRAMMAIRE
Le génitif • Les déterminants possessifs • *Can / Can't* • *Like*

21 **Complète les phrases avec *his*, *her* ou *their*.**

a. I like the Queen. I love ... hats!
b. Do you know Prince William's title? Yes, ... title is the Duke of Cambridge.
c. William and Kate are often in London. ... residence is Kensington Palace.
d. Princess Ann has two children. ... son is called Peter and ... daughter is called Zara.
e. Harry and Meghan have two dogs. ... names are Guy and Oz.

22 **Devine de quoi il s'agit.**

Ex. : *It's green and yellow. It's Jonathan's T-shirt.*

a. They're white and pointed.
b. It's pink and black.
c. It's red and Navy blue.
d. It's black. *(2 possible answers)*
e. It's round and yellow.
f. They are big and they float in the air.

23 Remets les mots dans l'ordre pour former des phrases.

a. is - grumpy - Grandma - a - Wintera - person
b. hair - Mike - got - black - has - Uncle
c. lovely - grandad - Alfred - a - is
d. cookies - can - wonderful - He - make
e. scary - is - Wulver - man - a
f. smile - Mrs Jones - got - a - lovely - has

24 Complète la réponse aux questions avec le mot entre parenthèses.

a. Who is Princess Charlotte? She is *(sister)*.
b. Who is Kate? She is *(William)*.
c. Who is Hobbes? It is *(Calvin)*.
d. What is Hogwarts? It's *(school)*.
e. Who is Vlad? He is *(Dracula)*.
f. Who is Wintera? She is *(the twins)*.

25 Écris ce que Fei Fei peut/sait faire et ce qu'elle ne peut/sait pas faire.
Ex. : *Fei Fei can't really make mooncakes.*

can + BV	*can't* + BV
- Ride a bike - Create a rocket - Plan a Moon mission	- Really make mooncakes - Go to the Moon at first - Fly her prototypes at first

26 Maintenant, écris ce que Fei Fei aime ou n'aime pas faire. Ex. : *Fei Fei likes drinking smoothies.*

❤	❤ (barré)
- Drink smoothies - Eat noodles - Write in her diary - Listen to legends - Do maths and physics - Explore the Moon	- Play with her stepbrother - Lose competitions - Forget her mother - Talk with her stepmother at first

LEXIQUE
La description physique • Les activités

27 Complète cette présentation des Indestructibles *(The Incredibles)*.

Do you know Bob Parr, Mr Incredible? He is very (≠ small)... and ... . Helen is his ... . She is ... and (≠ slow) ... . Her hair is ... . Violet is their ... . She has got long ... hair and she is (≠ stupid) ... . Dash and Jack-Jack are their ... . Jack-Jack is a baby, he is very ... and he is (≠ serious) ... . Dash is extremely (≠ slow) ... .

28 Nomme les parties du corps.

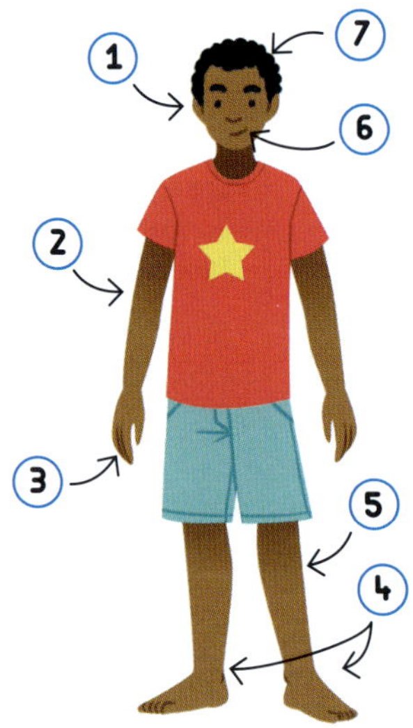

29 Complète les talents ou centres d'intérêt de chacun.

Tina is a musician: she can (a.) ... . She is sporty too: she can (b.) ... and (c.) ... . Her brother is creative: he loves (d.) ... and (e.) ... . They like ... television and ... to music.

a. b. c. d. e.

30 La description d'Edna Mode n'est pas tout à fait exacte : rétablis la vérité.

Edna Mode is a tall woman. She is beautiful. She has got curly blond hair. She has got a small nose. She has got a long dress.

UNIT 4 (pp. 70-87)

GRAMMAIRE

Le présent simple • Les adverbes de fréquence • *There is / There are* • Les questions

31 Avec tes amis, vous montez une pièce de théâtre : complète la description du décor avec *there is* ou *there are*.

The play takes place in a restaurant: ... four round tables, ... a counter on the left. On each table, ... a vase with flowers and a lamp. ... paintings on the wall. On the right ... two armchairs and a sofa. ... a huge television set in a corner.

32 Tu veux interroger sur la place des objets ou des personnes, quelles questions vas-tu poser ? Attention au singulier et au pluriel.

Ex. : *The teapot is on the table. Where is the teapot?*

a. The books are on the floor.
b. The paintings are on the wall.
c. The vase is in front of the window.
d. The lamp is behind Wallace's armchair.
e. Gromit is in the living room.

33 Le renseignement que tu veux est en caractère gras. Quelle question vas-tu poser ?

Ex. : *Wallace eats* ***crackers*** *with his tea.* → *What does Wallace eat with his tea?*

a. Wallace likes **cheese**.
b. Gromit reads **magazines**.
c. Wallace and Gromit drink **tea**.
d. There's **a black teapot**, **a bowl of sugar**, **a tray and a white tea cup** on the coffee table.
e. It's **5 PM**.

34 Mets le verbe à la bonne forme et ajoute l'adverbe entre parenthèses à l'endroit qui convient.

a. Amelia / go shopping around the world *(never)*.
b. Oliver / play video games *(always)*.
c. Mrs Jones / do the cooking *(never)*.
d. Mr Jones / do the cleaning *(always)*.
e. Amelia / take Morph out *(always)*.
f. Mr Jones / put the shopping away *(never)*.
g. Mrs Jones / do the gardening *(always)*.

35 Conjugue les verbes entre parenthèses à la bonne forme.

a. James is very lucky. Every day, he ... *(get)* up late and he ... *(have)* pancakes for breakfast.
b. He ... *(not / stay)* home alone because he always ... *(invite)* friends over for a movie. They sometimes ... *(go)* to the park but they ... *(not / stay)* long.
c. James ...*(not / have)* limited internet access so he often ... *(play)* games online with friends.
d. He ... *(not / tidy)* his bedroom, his parents are really cool, they ... *(not / care)*.

36 Trouve la question correspondant à chaque réponse.

a. No, he doesn't. Morph doesn't like curry spices.
b. Yes, he does. Morph sometimes transforms into a hamster.
c. Yes, he does. Morph often sleeps on the sofa.
d. No, he doesn't. Morph doesn't scare the twins' friends.
e. Yes, he does. Morph follows the twins everywhere.
f. No, he doesn't. Morph doesn't go swimming, he prefers flying.

37 Décris les habitudes de Janet.

Ex.: *She sometimes gets up late.*

sometimes

often

sometimes

always

often

never

LEXIQUE
Les lieux et objets de la maison • La localisation • Les actions quotidiennes

38 Devine de quelle pièce de la maison il s'agit.

a. The sofa and a television are in the ... .
b. The computer and the desk are in the ... .
c. The bath or the shower are in the ... .
d. The fridge and the oven are in the ... .
e. The car and the bikes are in the ... .
f. The bed and the toys are in the ... .
g. The trees and the flowers are in the ... .
h. The entrance door and the stairs are in the ... .

39 Devine les bons objets en fonction des pièces de la maison où ils se trouvent normalement.

a. The ... and the ... are in the dining room to sit and have dinner.
b. The ... is in the living room to watch films and play video games.
c. There's a ... in the living room to relax in front of the television.
d. There are ... on the wall to decorate the bedroom.
e. The milk is in the ..., in the kitchen.
f. There are TV ... on the coffee table in the living room.

40 Écris ce que tu fais à différents moments de la journée.

a. At 4 PM, I ...
b. At 7 AM, I ...
c. Between 5:30 and 6:30 PM, I ...
d. At 9:30 PM, I ...

41 Joue à l'interprète. Peux-tu traduire les éléments manquants ?

a.	stairs	...
b.	...	un bureau (pièce)
c.	...	la salle de bain
d.	...	un réfrigérateur
e.	...	une photo, une image
f.	an armchair	...
g.	...	un ordinateur
h.	...	la porte d'entrée

42 **Regarde la chambre d'Oliver et Amelia et retrouve de quoi ou de qui l'on parle.**

a. ... is on the red chair.
b. The ... is between the two windows.
c. The red and white ... are in front of Tim and next to the little table.
d. The ... is between the computer and the books on the desk.
e. The ... is on the floor and on the papers.
f. The green ... is under the desk.
g. ... is sitting on the bed behind Tim.
h. ... is sitting between Sophia and Tim.

UNIT 5 (pp. 88-105)

GRAMMAIRE

Les quantités • *Must / Mustn't* • *Be + V-ing* • Les prépositions

Pour parler des dates, on utilise les prépositions *on* ou *in* :

on + a day

We have a test on Monday.

in + a month / a year

Christmas is in December.

43 **Complète le dialogue avec la bonne préposition : *in* ou *on*.**

a. –When is your birthday? Is it ... June?
b. –No, it isn't. It's ... July. It's ... July the 15th. And yours? I think it's ... February, isn't it?
c. –Yes, it is. Do you know the exact date?
d. –I think it's ... the 8th, isn't it?
e. –No, not at all, it's ... the 21st.
f. –I must write it down not to forget! So your birthday is ... February, ... the 21st of February.
g. –And your birthday is ... July, ... the 15th of July!

44 **Voici une liste de courses. Écris les questions que tu dois poser pour connaître les prix. Fais attention à la conjugaison de *be*.**

biscuits - a bottle of Coke - a cupcake - a cheeseburger - French fries

a. ... the biscuits?
b. ... a bottle of Coke?
c. ... a cupcake?
d. ... a cheeseburger?
e. ... French fries?

Pour indiquer une quantité :

A lot of + noun

On l'emploie pour parler d'une grande quantité.

There's a lot of fruit and a lot of sugar on my cake.

Some / Any

Si la quantité n'est pas définie (une certaine quantité), on emploie ***some*** dans une affirmation et ***any*** dans une négation.

Have some tea!

No, you can't have any sweets.

45 **Complète les phrases avec *a lot of*, *some* ou *any*.**

a. –There are ... sweets in the box. You can have ....
b. –Look! There are no sweets left in the box so you can't have ...
c. DAVE: –Mum, can I have ... Coke, please?
MOTHER: –There's a lot of fruit juice, you can have some. But there's no Coke, sorry! You can't have any!
d. WILLIAM: –Is there ... milk left?
KATE: –No, we need to buy ...
WILLIAM: –What else do we need?
KATE: –Buy ... flour and ... eggs too, we can make pancakes this afternoon!
WILLIAM: –Great idea!

46 **À la maison, tes parents établissent les règles. Essaie de les mémoriser... et complète avec *must* ou *mustn't*.**

a. We ... do our homework when we come back from school.
b. We ... watch TV before our homework is finished.

c. We … spend too much time on the computer.
d. We … help our parents in the kitchen to make dinner.

47 Voici la liste de courses pour ton anniversaire. Que dois-tu acheter ? Que dois-tu ne pas acheter ?

48 Ta mère aimerait que tu l'aides dans le jardin. Tu refuses en lui expliquant combien tu es occupé(e).

–Can you come and help me, please?
–Sorry Mum, I can't, I'm busy at the moment, I *(do)* … my homework.
–Come on! You *(not/do)* … any work. You *(listen)* … to music!
–No, Mum. I *(do)* …. my Spanish. Ask Jimmy to help you!
–He can't. He *(help)* …. with his friend Alex. They *(clean up)* … the community park.

49 Formule au moins 6 interdictions ou obligations lisibles sur ce panneau.

Ex. : *You mustn't sleep at night in the park.*

50 Quel est ton programme pour ce week-end ?

I *(have)* … a busy weekend!
I *(go)* … to the swimming pool on Saturday morning, then, at lunch time, I *(see)* … Kate and Ben at the shopping centre. In the afternoon, we *(go)* … to the ice rink. We *(meet)* … other friends there. In the evening, Tim *(organise)* … a party at his place. I *(take)* … some good music!

LEXIQUE

La nourriture • Les émotions • Les activités de fêtes

51 Établis une liste de courses au rayon fruits et légumes aussi longue que possible.

52 Devine de quel aliment il s'agit.

a. You can make a sandwich with them: … and …
b. You can spell it with 7 letters, the first letter is y: …
c. It is a drink made with fruit: …
d. You can have them for a picnic: a packet of …
e. It's brown or black, sometimes white and you eat a lot at Christmas and at Easter: …
f. You eat a big one for a special occasion: …

53 Trouve tout ce que tu dois faire pour avoir un bel anniversaire.

You must … a party, … cards to … your friends, … food and drinks, … some good music, … the decorations and of course, … your parents! Now they can …. the candles and you can … your birthday!

54 Quelle émoticône correspond à chacun des adjectifs suivants ?

a. excited - b. annoyed - c. surprised - d. mocking - e. angry

UNIT 6 (pp. 106-123)

GRAMMAIRE
Le prétérit • *Would like to* + BV

55 Maya et sa mère prévoient leur programme du week-end prochain. Complète la conversation en utilisant *would like to* + BV. Choisis le verbe qui convient parmi la liste suivante :
meet - eat - do - go - invite - drink

a. –Mum, I ... to the cinema this week-end. The new Avengers is on!
b. –Ok Maya. Good idea. What else ...?
c. –Mmmh, let me think, I ... my friends on Sunday.
d. –Why not? We can invite them for lunch then. What (they) ...?
e. –Pizzas of course! And I'm sure they ... Coke.
f. –And fruit juice! (you) ... our new neighbours' son?
–Well, not really. But if you insist...

56 Choisis les activités que tu aimerais faire ou non pendant ton prochain camp de vacances.
Ex. : *I wouldn't like to go fishing.*

Activities	yes	no
- Go fishing	x	
- Go canoeing		
- Visit museums		
- Take part in storytelling		
- Ride a quad		
- Play outdoor games		
- Go hiking		
- Make jewels		
- Do papercraft		

57 Complète par la forme correcte de *be* au passé : *was / wasn't* ou *were / weren't* ?

a. I ... at school yesterday because I ... ill.
b. When she ... a kid, my mother ... a very good football player.
c. Last July, my family and I ... in London for a week. It ... great.
d. Did you know that the rock band Queen ... American? They ... an English band of course!
e. – "How ... your birthday party?"
– "Great! There ... good music and there ... a lot of sweets to eat!"

58 Complète l'histoire de la Tour de Londres : écris les verbes au passé.

In the 1070s William the Conqueror *(start)* ... to build a fortress in East London. It *(take)* ... about 20 years to finish it. The medieval kings *(transform)* ... it into a large and strong castle. Masons *(bring)* ... stone from Normandy to build the central White Tower. Kings and Queens *(use)* ... the fortress to protect their possessions. They *(live)* ... in luxurious apartments. It *(become)* ... a prison during the Tudor age and some famous people *(be)* ... executed there, like Anne Boleyn.

59 Ton amie Sarah revient des États-Unis. Pose-lui des questions sur son voyage. Elle te répond avec des phrases courtes.
Ex. : *Go by plane?* ✓ *Did you go by plane, Sarah? Yes, I did.*

Stay at a hotel? ✓ Eat bagels? ✓
Visit Chicago? ✓ See the White House? ✗
Watch an NBA match? ✗ Enthusiastic about New York? ✓

60 Ses réponses t'ont rendu(e) très curieux(se) et tu voudrais maintenant plus de détails. Complète la conversation avec Sarah.

a. –How long *(you / stay)* ... in Chicago?
b. –I only *(stay)* ... for 2 days because the weather *(be / not)* ... good.
c. –Where *(you / go)* ... next?
d. –We *(take)* ... a plane to San Francisco. And that *(be)* ... great!
e. –What *(you / do)* ... there?
f. –Lots of things. We *(go)* ... to the waterfront and we *(eat)* ... fresh crab. We *(drive)* ... across the Golden Gate Bridge of course! We *(see)* ... Alcatraz Island in the distance but we *(not / go)* ... there!

LEXIQUE
Les transports • Le tourisme • Se repérer dans l'espace

61 Quelle est la direction opposée ?

a. North - b. East - c. South East
d. North East - e. On the right

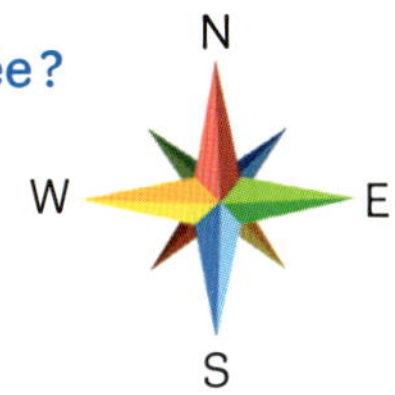

62 Quelles activités peux-tu faire lorsque tu visites une ville ? Relie chaque verbe au bon complément.

a. visit	1. a souvenir
b. do	2. a museum
c. buy	3. in a park
d. take	4. the town
e. discover	5. to the theatre
f. walk	6. down the river
g. go	7. photos
h. sail	8. some shopping

63 Quel est le kit du parfait touriste ? Retrouve les mots en mettant les lettres dans l'ordre.

a. K-P-A-B-A-C-C-K = …
b. A-M-P = …
c. M-E-R-C-A-A = …
d. F-L-A-T-L-E-E = …

64 Joue à l'interprète. Traduis les éléments manquants.

a.	…	un pont
b.	a wheel	…
c.	…	une tour
d.	…	un stade
e.	…	un toit
f.	jewels	…
g.	…	un château
h.	…	une rivière

65 Retrouve les moyens de transport correspondant à ces définitions.

a. I'm usually black in London and yellow in New York: I am a …
b. I can transport passengers and I am red in London: I am a …
c. I transport passengers under cities like London, Paris, New York, Lyon: I am the …
d. I need no petrol, only strong legs: I am a …

UNIT 7 (pp. 124-137)

GRAMMAIRE
Faire des suggestions, des propositions • *Will* + BV

66 Exprime les suggestions suivantes en utilisant *Why not* + BV…? ou *What about* + *V-ing*…? ou *Let's* + BV…!

–… having lunch outside, it's warm and sunny!
–… use the new camping chairs?
–Yes! Good idea! … take them out of the shed.
–And … start a barbecue?
–Yes, … grilling pork chops?
–Ok! Then … go to the butcher's!

67 Tu élabores avec tes amis un programme d'activité pour le week-end prochain. Chacun suggère quelque chose à faire. Sers-toi des étiquettes en couleur.

- *What about + V-ing?*
- *Why not + BV?*
- *Let's + BV (decision made)!*

hiking | badminton | tent | a castle
in a lake | in a lake | treasure hunt
a bonfire | a bike ride | pizza and bagels

68 Bientôt les vacances ! Mais la météo pour la semaine prochaine n'est pas très bonne. Imagine ce que ta famille et toi ferez (= *will do*). Voici quelques suggestions :
television - latest "Wimpy Kid" book - cupcakes - music - cards - yoga
I think …

Monday	Tuesday	Wednesday	Thursday	Friday	Saturday	Sunday

69 Mr et Mrs Grant sont en colère contre leurs enfants. et veulent que les choses changent. Les enfants font des promesses. Choisis un verbe de la liste et écris-le à la forme correcte : *call - clean - cook - do - take - tidy - see*

TIM: – OK, I ... my room and I ... the shower. Promise!

JESS: – I ... the dog out this evening and I ... my homework before 6 PM. Promise!

ABY: – I ... dinner and ... Grandma. Promise!

MR AND MRS GRANT: – OK, we ...!

LEXIQUE

Les loisirs • Les sports • Les lieux de villégiature

70 Quels sports pratiquent ces personnes?

a. They play with a club and a small white ball.

b. Lisa loves playing this game with her friends.

c. Tom does this sport with his friends in a special park with ramps.

d. It's quite dangerous, especially on high cliffs or rocks.

e. It's fun on the beach with big waves!

f. My parents love walking in the countryside or he mountains.

g. I often go on the river with my sister: we row in turns.

h. My dad goes to the river too. He can wait for hours on the riverside or in his boat.

i. I like going on the river too or in the sea and I love speed!

71 Retrouve les lieux décrits.

a. A place with lots of trees.

b. There is snow in the winter and you can ski there.

c. You can set up your tent there.

d. There is sand and you can sunbathe and relax.

e. In Scotland it's called a loch.

72 Devine de quelle activité il s'agit.

a. Roald Dahl was very good at it.

b. We do it during our music lessons.

c. We can have it at night when camping.

d. I organised one in the park for my birthday party.

e. We practise it at school in the drama hall.

UNIT 8 (pp. 138-147)

GRAMMAIRE

Le prétérit • Les marqueurs de temps et les mots de liaison

73 Est-ce que tu te souviens bien de la légende d'Arthur? Si nécessaire, rétablis la vérité ou donne des précisions.

Ex. : *Was Merlin a king? No, he wasn't. (He was a magician.)*

a. Did he live in a city?

b. Did Sir Hector adopt Arthur?

c. Was Kay Arthur's cousin?

d. Did Arthur enjoy Merlin's lessons?

e. Were the knights stronger than Arthur?

f. Did Arthur keep Excalibur?

g. Did he become famous?

74 Complète la carte postale de Amelia. Choisis le bon verbe dans la liste et écris-le au prétérit.

Go - be (2) - have - cycle - not/see - take - visit

Dear Grandma,

We're on holiday in New York! Yesterday we ... a fantastic time. We ... to Central Park and we ... in the alleys. There ... a lot of people there! Dad ... photos.

Then we ... the Empire State Building. The view from the top ... amazing! But we ... King Kong!

Hope you're fine!

See you soon,

Millie

75 Complète les phrases avec le mot ou l'expression qui convient dans la liste suivante.

And - at first - but - because - so - then

She went to the park ... she played with her friends. ... they played rounders, ... they had a game of football with the boys. ... it started to rain ... they decided to go to Jill's ... watch a film. ... Jill's mother refused ... her baby was asleep. ... they went to the cinema.

76 Réponds au questionnaire sur les Jones.

Ex. : *Who did the twins visit their new school with?*
The twins visited their new school with Tim and Sophia.

a. Which room did they see?
b. What did Mr. Jones need for cooking?
c. Where did Oliver buy bananas?
d. Where did the twins celebrate their birthday?
e. What did the schoolchildren see in the Natural Science Museum?
f. What activity did they do at the adventure park?
g. Who filmed them?

LEXIQUE
Les personnages • Les animaux et créatures • La personnalité • Les accessoires

77 Retrouve les paires.

a. a prince	1. a magic wand
b. a warrior	2. a princess
c. elves	3. a knight
d. a king	4. bows & arrows
e. a magician	5. a broom and a bat
f. a queen	6. cute with small wings
g. a witch	7. a sword
h. a fairy	8. a shield

78 Retrouve qui vit où.

a. An ogre lives in a ...
b. ... and ... live in palaces.
c. ... and fairies live in the forest.
d. Cinderella lived in a .... When she married the ... , they lived in ...

79 Trouve le bon adjectif pour qualifier leur personnalité.

a. King Arthur was (= courageous) ...
b. Snow White was (≠ ugly) ... and her prince was (= good-looking) ...
c. Dudley Dursley is a very unpleasant boy, he is (≠ polite) ... and cruel.
d. The Grinch is very (= irritable) ...
e. Olaf is always very (affectionate) ... with Elsa but Prince Hans is (= nasty) ...
f. Grandpa Joe is very (= he gives a lot, he is not selfish) ... with Charlie.

80 Fais la liste de tous les noms d'animaux que tu as rencontrés dans l'unité 8 et dans ton manuel.

Crédits iconographiques

Couverture: FreePik - **p.16:** Prod DB © Walt Disney Animation Studios - Walt Disney Pictures/DR – **p.20:** Stinger/UK Home Office/AFP - **p.22:** Hagen Hopkins/Getty Images Asiapac; Afp Photo/Franck Fife; Sportsfile/Corbis via Getty Images); AP Photo/Dita Alangkara)/sipapress - **p.23:** rue des archives; Photo Josse/Leemage; SunsetBox/AllPix/Aurimages; Hurford Brown Debra/Camera Press/ABACA - **p.27:** Archives du 7e Art/Twentieth Century Fox Animation/photo12; Jordan Strauss/AP/SIPA; Chris Ashford/CAMERAPRESS/GAMMA-RAPHO; Pandora via Bestimage - **p.30:** Prod DB © Matt Groening 20th Century Fox/DR; Courtesy Walt Disney Productions/Everett/Rue des Archives - **p.31:** Prod DB © Orion-Paramont/DR; Prod DB © Warner Bros/DR; Prod DB © BBC Wales - Hartswood Films - Masterpiece Theatre/DR; Jason Merritt/Getty Images/ AFP – **p.32:** Gail Hedgpetha/EyeEm/Getty Images; Izusek/Photo12 - **p.34:** istockphoto/getty - **p.37:** Compassionate Eye Foundation/Chris Ryan/ Getty Images - **p.38:** Adrian Sherratt/Alamy Stock Photo/Hemis; **p.38:** First day at Secondary school © BBC - **p.40:** Courtesy of Halewood Academy (Liverpool)/Gary Evans - **p.41:** © Warner Bros/DR; Collection Christophel; Prod DB © Warner Bros. Pictures - Heyday Films /DR; Prod DB © Warner Bros/DR; Prod DB © Warner Bros/DR - **p.43:** photo12/Alamy; photo12/Alamy; Catchlight Visual Services/Alamy Stock Photo/ Hemis - **p.44:** Photo12/Alamy; Roy Peters/Report Digital-REA; Graham Oliver/Juices Images/Photononstop; Robert Daly/plainpicture; Juices Images/Photononstop; fotolia; photononstop - **p.45:** True Images/Alamy/Hemis - CALVIN AND HOBBES © 1988 Watterson. Reprinted with permission of ANDREWS MCMEEL SYNDICATION. All rights reserved; CALVIN AND HOBBES © 1992 Watterson. Reprinted with permission of ANDREWS MCMEEL SYNDICATION. All rights reserved - **p.48:** Prod DB © Warner Bros. - J.K. Rowling/DR - **p.50:** Roy Peters/Report Digital/REA Alamy/Steve Speller/Photo12; - **p.52:** Columbia Pictures/Sony Pictures Entertainment/BBQ_DFY/Aurimages - **p.54:** PA Photos/ABACA - **p.55:** Chris Jackson/Getty Images; Alpha Press/Maxppp; Gillard/Camerapress/Gamma; Ferrari/Starface; 1000credit - **p.56:** Prod DB © Sony Pictures Animation - Columbia Pictures - LStar Capital/DR; 2015 CTMG/Sony Pictures/Columbia Pictures; Prod DB © Sony Pictures Animation - Columbia Pictures - LStar Capital/DR; Prod DB © Sony Pictures Animation - Columbia Pictures - LStar Capital/DR; Prod DB © Sony Pictures Animation - Columbia Pictures - LStar Capital/DRht mike; 2015 CTMG/Sony Pictures/Columbia Pictures; Prod DB © Sony Pictures Animation Columbia Pictures - LStar Capital/DR - **p.57:** Prod DB © Sony Pictures Animation - Columbia Pictures - LStar Capital/DR; Prod DB © Sony Pictures Animation - Columbia Pictures - LStar Capital/DR; Suzette Rothlisberger/Getty Images - **p.58**: Twentieth Century-Fox Film/The Kobal Collection/Aurimages - **p.59:** Alamy/Hemis - **p.62:** photo12; World History Archive/Aurimages; Collection Dagli Orti/Collection Privée/Philip Mould /Aurimages; World History Archive/Aurimages; Bridgeman Images/Leemage; Musée du Louvre Paris/Gianni Dagli Orti/Aurimages; Granger Coll NY/Aurimages; The Granger Coll NY/Aurimages; The Granger Coll NY/Aurimages; The Granger Coll NY/Aurimages; The Granger Coll NY/Aurimages; Karwai Tang/ WireImage/Getty Images; Everett Collection//Rue des Archives; Prod DB © Blue Sky - 20th Century Fox/DR; Walt Disney Pictures/Pixar Animation Studios. All Rights Reserved/Prod DB;Walt Disney Pictures/Courtesy/Everett Collection/Aurimages - **p.63:** Prod DB © Warner Bros./DR; **p.63:** Draw my life! Matilda Ramsay © BBC- **p.66:** Picture Press Europe/SIPA; Hussein Anwar/SIPA; Hussein Anwar/SIPA - **p.67:** Frederic Haslin /Corbis via Getty Images – **p.68:** Walt Disney Pictures/courtesy Everett Collection/Aurimages - **p.70:** georgeclerk/Getty Images - **p.72:** © SevenSuperGirls - **p.73:** Andreas von Einsiedel/Getty Images; Zoonar GmbH/Alamy/Hemis - **p.74:** Prod DB © Aardman - DreamWorks/DR - **p.75**: Adam Woolfitt/ afp; Photo12/Alamy; Frances Stéphane/Hemis.fr; GIANCARLO ZEMA DESIGN GROUP - **p.76:** istockphoto/Getty Images; Grady: Damian/Getty Images - **p.77:** Pete Niesen/Alamy/Hemis; Robert Harding/Hemis.fr; deby66y/shutterstock; John Davidson Photos/Alamy/Hemis - **p.81:** istock; masterfile; Prod DB © Walt Disney/DR – **p.85:** Shutterstock - **p.88:** prod db - **p.91:** Alamy/Simon Dack/Photo12 - **p.92:** James Veysey/ Camerapress/Gamma-Rapho; Chris Ashford/Camerapress/Gamma-Rapho; Mike Rosenthal/Getty Images - **p.95:** Richard Watkins/Alamy/Hemis - **p.97:** Prod DB © Pixar Animation Studios - Walt Disney Pictures/DR; Prod DB © Pixar Animation Studios - Walt Disney Pictures/DR; Prod DB © Pixar Animation Studios - Walt Disney Pictures/DR; Prod DB © Pixar Animation Studios - Walt Disney Pictures/DR - **p.98:** Bauer-Griffin/GC Images/ Getty Images; Paul Edwards - WPA Pool/Getty Images; AP Photo/Peter Morrison/Sipa; Justin Tallis - WPA Pool/Getty Images; Owen Humphreys - WPA Pool/Getty Images; George Rogers/SIPA; Morgan/SIPA; Samir Hussein/WireImage/Getty Images - **p.99:** Selva/Leemage - **p.106:** Luca Locatelli/INSTITUTE - **p.109:** Sasse/LAIF-REA - **p.111**: Grant Rooney Premium/Alamy Stock Photo; Christer Fredriksson/Lonely Planet Images / Getty Images; istockphoto/Getty Images; istockphotos/Getty Images; Bibikow Walter/Hemis.fr; Ross D. Franklin/AP/SIPA; istockpphotos/Getty Images - **p.112:** Alamy/GRANT ROONEY PREMIUM/Photo12 - **p.113:** Rudi Van Starrex/Getty Images - **p.115:** AP Photo/Matt Marto/sipa - **p.120:** © CChaumet - **p.124**: Getty Images - **p.126:** Peter Dench/Getty Images Reportage - **p.128:** longlakecamp - **p.129:** From SISTERS, by Raina Telgemeier. Published by Graphix, an imprint of Scholastic, Inc. Copyright © 2014 by Raina Telgemeier used by permission. - **p.133:** Hill Street Studios/Blend Images RM/agefotostock - **p.136:** Kuttig - RF - Kids/Alamy/Hemis - **p.138:** ImageBroker/ Hemis.fr - p.141: TCD; Walt Disney Pictures/The Kobal Collection/Aurimages - **p.142:** iStock/Getty Images Plus - **p.143:** christopheL; istockphoto - **p.150:** jklmon; PHOTO12/ALAMY - Brent Hofacker/Shutterstock - **p.152**: AFP photo/Leon Neal - **p.153:** Matthew Chattle/Alamy/Hemis – **p.154:** Brooke Slezak/Getty Images – **p.155:** Artwork courtesy of the Norman Rockwell family agency; Alex Segre/Alamy/Hemis; Pawel Libera/LightRocket via Getty Images - **p.156:** Peter Muhly/Alamy/Hemis; W. G. Murray/ Alamy/Hemis; Maurizio Rellini/Sime/Photononstop - **p.157:** Sipa press; Alamy/photo12 - **p.158:** Michael Ochs Archives/Getty Images; Michael Ochs Archives/Getty Images - **p.159:** Trae Patton/NBC/NBCU Photo Bank via Getty Images; Frank Maddocks; MTV/Getty Images /AFP - **p.160:** The British Library Board/Leemage; Leemage; North Wind Pictures/Leemage; GL Archive/Alamy Stock Photo/Hemis; Andreviegas/Getty Images/Premium Access; Liquid Light/Alamy Stock Photo; Mark Phillips/Alamy Stock Photo - **p.161**: Alamy/photo12; Luisa Ricciarini/Leemage; Leemage; Tim Graham Picture Library/Getty Images - **p.162:** Akg-images; The Huntington Library, Art Collections & Botanical Gardens/ Bridgeman Images; Hank Walker/The LIFE Picture Collection/Getty Images; Superstock/Leemage; PVDE/ Bridgeman Images; Ewing Galloway/UIG/Leemage; Akg-images - **p.163:** Schulmann-Sachs/AFP; Bachrach/Getty Images; PONO PRESSE INTERNATIONALE/GAMMA-RAPHO; Pete Souza/The Image Works/Roger-Viollet; Simon Bruty/Sports Illustrated/Getty Images; UIG/Leemage; Nasa; Nasa; Rick Friedman/Corbis via Getty Images; AP Photo/Paul Sancya/Sipa; Joshua Roberts/Getty Images; Gabrielle Lurie/The San Francisco Chronicle via Getty Images – **p.164:** Kokkai Ng/Getty Images - **p.166:** Sony Pictures Releasing /Courtesy Everett Collection/Aurimages; © 2020– **p.167-168:** Netflix, Inc; Pixar Animation Studios/Walt Disney Pictures/BBQ_DFY/Aurimages; Walt Disney/courtesy Everett Collection/Aurimages - **p.171:** Alamy/Kypros/Photo12 – **p.172:** Rudy Sulgan/Getty Images – **p.174:** Tony Evans/Getty Images; Photo 12/Alamy/Gary E. Perkin

Pour les autres images: ©fotolia/©istock/©Adobe/©Freepik

Crédits des vidéos

p. 38 : First day at Secondary school © BBC
p. 63 : Draw my life! Matilda Ramsay © BBC
p. 72 : © SevenSuperGirls

Achevé d'imprimer en France par Clerc en juillet 2021
Dépôt légal : Avril 2021 - N° d'éditeur MAGSI20201014

I BET YOU CAN CELEBRATE!

A school year of holidays!

Workbook p. 142-143

Back to school!

OCTOBER

31st HALLOWEEN

Halloween is an ancient Celtic festival. Today, children in costumes go from house to house and say "trick or treat" to get sweets! They carve jack o'lanterns, too!

NOVEMBER

THANKSGIVING

This celebration honours Native Americans who offered food to the first Europeans in America. Families eat a big dinner with turkey, sweet potatoes and pumpkin pie.

DECEMBER

25th CHRISTMAS DAY

It's a religious holiday and a cultural phenomenon! People in English-speaking countries decorate their houses with Christmas trees and stockings and send Christmas cards.

JANUARY

1st NEW YEAR'S DAY

It's the first day of a new year and a day for new resolutions! On New Year's Eve, people gather in NYC's Times Square to watch the ball drop and bring in the new year.

FEBRUARY

14th VALENTINE'S DAY

Love is celebrated today! People send cards (or e-cards) and give chocolate and roses to their loved ones. In the US, children send cards to everyone in their class.

MARCH

SHROVE TUESDAY

Better known as Pancake Day! It's the last day before "Lent" (fasting before Easter). People eat pancakes! In the UK, there are pancake races. It can also fall in February!

MARCH

17th SAINT PATRICK'S DAY

Saint Patrick's Day is a cultural and religious celebration. Irish people all around the world celebrate Saint Patrick (385-461), the patron saint of Ireland.

APRIL

1st APRIL FOOLS' DAY

Today you can play silly jokes on your family and friends. Change the sugar to salt or put a funny sign on your friend's back and say "April Fools!" (but not in English class, of course)!

EASTER

Easter is a religious celebration. The "Easter Bunny" hides chocolate eggs in the garden. On Easter Sunday, children look for them and play outside. It can also fall in March.

MAY

1st MAY DAY

In some parts of the UK, people dance around the village maypole decorated with flowers. People also celebrate and honour workers around the world.

JUNE

9th TROOPING THE COLOUR

Today is Queen Elizabeth's official birthday! But her real birthday is on April 21st. From Buckingham Palace, the Queen and her family watch a parade in her honour.

JULY

4th INDEPENDENCE DAY (US)

America celebrates the signature of the Declaration of Independence on July 4th, 1776. Americans celebrate with parades, barbecues and fireworks!

School's out for the summer!

I Bet You Can express your feelings

I feel scared.
I'm afraid.
That's scary.

I'm silly.
I'm funny.

I'm furious.
I'm mad!

I'm sorry.
Sorry: my bus was late!
Sorry I'm late.

I feel surprised.
Really? That's incredible!
I can't believe it!

I'm angry.
I don't like that.

I feel sick.
I'm ill.
I don't feel well.

I'm proud.
I can do it!
Wow, I did it!

I feel sad.
I'm a bit upset.

I feel sleepy.
I want to sleep.
I'm very tired.

I feel happy.
I'm fine... I'm great...
I feel good.

I feel disappointed.
Oh, no!
That's too bad...

I'm nervous.
I'm shy.

I feel excited.
That's great!